Map of Plymouth area by Samuel de Champlain, 1604

MOURT'S RELATION:

A JOURNAL OF THE PILGRIMS OF PLYMOUTH

MOURT'S RELATION: A JOURNAL OF THE PILGRIMS OF PLYMOUTH

EDITED BY

JORDAN D. FIORE
PROFESSOR OF HISTORY
BRIDGEWATER STATE COLLEGE

PLYMOUTH ROCK FOUNDATION
PLYMOUTH, MASSACHUSETTS
1985

Copyright © 1985
by the Plymouth Rock Foundation
Plymouth, Massachusetts 02360

Published by
THE PLYMOUTH ROCK FOUNDATION

Set in Baskerville typeface by Thoburn Press
Tyler, Texas

Printed by Iversen-Norman Associates
Irvington-on-Hudson, New York

ISBN 0-942516-07-9

TABLE OF CONTENTS

MOURT'S
RELATION:
A JOURNAL
OF THE
PILGRIMS OF
PLYMOUTH

TABLE OF
CONTENTS

ILLUSTRATIONS AND MAPS

PREFACE

This reprint of the book popularly known as *Mourt's Relation* represents the first annotated edition with modernized spelling and punctuation in almost one hundred and fifty years. Young's edition of 1841, with modernized spelling and punctuation, and Dexter's edition of 1865, which kept the original spelling and punctuation, were the last major attempts at an annotated work. The editor hopes that he has utilized the best work of both editors and has added many of his own notes.

The importance of this work is discussed in the historical essay that follows. As the first printed work by and about the original Pilgrims, the historical importance of the work is widely recognized. The editor hopes that he has made it more readable for the modern student.

The editor is indebted to many persons for this book. John G. Talcott, Jr., of Plymouth, who heads the Plymouth Rock Foundation, has generously supplied funds and encouragement to complete the work. Rus Walton, the director of the Foundation, has guided it through the publication process and to him the editor is grateful.

Several persons have read the transcript and have made valuable suggestions, many of which have been accepted and utilized. Dr. George A. Horner, Professor Emeritus of Anthropology at Bridgewater State College, who is an expert on the history and folklore of New England Indians, Dr. Harry Ward, Professor of History at the University of Richmond and the author of several books in United States colonial history, the late Rose T. Briggs, former director of the Pilgrim Society in Plymouth, and my esteemed colleague at Bridgewater State College, Professor Jean F. Stonehouse, who has served as reader, critic, and advisor on the work, have been particularly helpful.

Others who encouraged the work and offered advice were the members of the executive committee of the Pilgrim Society, the Fellows of that Society and especially H. Hobart Holly, the Senior Fellow, and students in several of my seminars on the Pilgrims and Plymouth Colony at Bridgewater State College.

Several typists have struggled with the editor's poor handiwork to produce the final manuscript. Particular thanks go to Mrs. Kathleen G. Economos and Mrs. Dorothy A. Hoff for their assistance in this aspect of the work.

The editor takes full responsibility for errors, omissions, and any judgments that may be contrary to those generally accepted. This entire project has been a labor of love.

J.D.F.

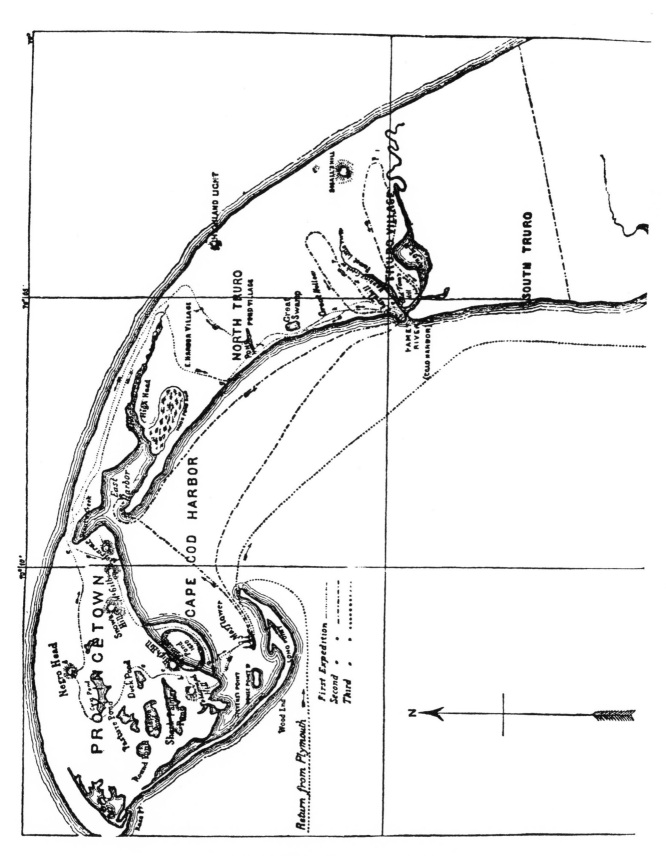

Map of the Pilgrims' Exploration of Cape Cod,
from Dexter's Edition of *Mourt's Relation*

A History of
Mourt's Relation

To begin with, the Pilgrim Fathers were ever mindful of their place in history. Although they were a small, modest, and unassuming band and probably not much of a force in their own day, these Pilgrims were very much aware of their past and of their responsibilities toward their friends in England and Holland, as well as to their own posterity. They were excellent record-keepers as well. The large amount of primary material about this small group is almost unparalleled in any microcosm of society in their age.

In the fall of 1621 the survivors of that terrible first winter in Plymouth were quite content with their lives. After the general sickness was over, those who survived gradually regained their health and strength. They had planted and gathered in a good crop, celebrated their famous Thanksgiving feast, and gathered lumber and furs to send to England to reduce their debts. Now they hoped that their creditors and investors would send them more supplies and help and that some of the Pilgrims who had been forced to return to England when the *Speedwell* turned back would join their friends in Plymouth.

When the *Fortune* arrived from England in the fall of 1621, new settlers came, but there were no supplies. Although the Pilgrims were pleased to see some old friends and the new settlers, Bradford commented that many of his colleagues wished that "many of them had been of better condition, and all of them better provided with provisions."

Among those who came on the *Fortune* was Robert Cushman, deacon of the congregation in Leyden, who had started out with the Pilgrims in 1620 but returned on the *Speedwell*. He stayed in Plymouth for a month and while there delivered one of the few Pilgrim sermons extant on "The Danger of Self Love."

Governor William Bradford kept a daily journal or diary during the first year in Plymouth. Although this has long been lost, we know that it existed because the Reverend Thomas Prince quoted frequently from it in his *Annals*, which covered the period to 1633, and which was first published in 1636. From that journal and probably from other notes and their memories, William Bradford and Edward Winslow reconstructed the account of this first year at Plymouth and gave it to Cushman so that information would be disseminated in London.

The reasons for writing this pamphlet are obvious. Bradford and Winslow hoped through this account to convince the investors that their money had been well-spent, and they wished to let them know that they had been busy and had accomplished

MOURT'S
RELATION:
A JOURNAL
OF THE
PILGRIMS OF
PLYMOUTH

A HISTORY OF
MOURT'S
RELATION

much in that first year. In addition, they hoped to induce others among their friends to come over and to share their bounty. It was probably not their intention to print the account in book form, but the decision to do so was wisely made in London by those who saw the excellent propaganda that it contained.

Robert Cushman's return trip to England on the *Fortune* was not uneventful. The ship was captured by a French vessel, and all of the goods which were the result of a year's labor by the Pilgrims were confiscated. Cushman was imprisoned for a few months, but he finally reached London. Here he sought out George Morton, a loyal Pilgrim and Bradford's good friend, who undoubtedly arranged the publication of the book and wrote a short introduction.

The book was finally published as *A Relation or Journal of the Beginnings and Proceedings of the English Plantation Settled at Plymouth in New England, by Certain English Adventurers Both Merchants and Others* . . . and goes on for twenty more lines. Mercifully, the name was shortened to *Mourt's Relation* by the Reverend Thomas Prince, and it is generally known by that name today. Who the printer was we do not know, for London in 1622 had a number of printers who might have produced the book on short notice. The imprint for the pamphlet on the title page lists London as the place of publication and states that the pamphlets were "Printed for John Bellamie, and are to be sold at his shop at the two greyhounds in Cornhill near the Royal Exchange."

The original pamphlet is about 7½ inches high and 5½ inches wide. It contains six preliminary leaves and 72 pages of text. Copies of the first edition are rare, but there have been many imprints including several excellent facsimile printings.

The work is unsigned, although the authorship of several parts is indicated by initials. The author of each part may be rather easily identified by internal evidence. The bulk of the published work is in the accounts prepared by Bradford and Winslow.

The pamphlet opens with a dedication "To His Much Respected Friend, Mr. I. P." "I. P." was John Peirce, London merchant who had helped the Leyden Separatists to go to the New World and in whose name they were granted their first patent. The dedication was signed "R. G.," a typographical error for "R. C.," or Robert Cushman.

Cushman wrote:

> As for the poor relation, I pray you to accept it, as being writ by the several actors themselves, after their plain and rude manner, therefore doubt nothing of the truth thereof; if it be defective in any thing, it is their ignorance, that are better acquainted with planting than writing.

He signed the dedication "Yours in the way of friendship."

The introduction, "To the Reader," was signed "G. Mourt," another typographical error. Again the internal evidence is enough to convince the reader that "G. Mourt" was George Morton. Morton was in London in 1622; he wrote that the authors are "my both known and faithful friends," and he talks of his desire to join his friends in Plymouth, which he did in the following year. The relationship between Morton and Bradford was to be closer. Bradford married for his second wife Morton's sister-in-law, and when Morton died in 1624, Bradford was responsible for raising his eldest son, the famous chronicler of Plymouth Colony, Nathaniel Morton.

Next in the pamphlet is a letter from John Robinson, their pastor in Leyden, signed "I. R." and entitled "Certain Useful Advertisements Sent in a Letter Written by a Discreet Friend unto its Planters in New England. . . ." The letter, originally written in July 1620, before the Mayflower voyage, warned the Pilgrims to make their peace with God and themselves," to provide for peace with all men what in us lieth, especially with our associates," to keep from giving offense to others, to work for the general good, and, finally, when they became "a body politick," to elect the best officials to lead them.

The next section is the heart of the book, some forty pages of text, which was obviously the work of William Bradford. This was a straight narrative, an account of the colony beginning with the sailing from Plymouth, England on September 6, 1620 (o.s.), and then almost a day-by-day account of the settlement, the landing, the exploration of Cape Cod, the search for a permanent site, the hardships of the first winter, the coming of Samoset and Tisquantum (Squanto), the peace treaty with Massasoit, and finally the election of John Carver as governor later in March 1621. Here we have also the account of the Mayflower Compact, and the first printing of the text of that milestone.

But at the same time the greatest value of this section is in the detail of geographical, ecological, and ethnographical information. Bradford had a good retentive memory. To this day it is not difficult to cover much of the same ground that the Pilgrims roved. In addition, Bradford gave a detailed account of the landscape; the hills, the dunes, the bays, the streams, the soil, all came in for examination. And we learn a great deal about the fish and shellfish, the wild fruit, the plants and the animals of the area.

A few years earlier John Smith had performed a good service in describing New England, and William Bradford added to this description. More than a dozen years later William Wood added to our knowledge, but the person who had read Bradford's account was already familiar with much of the flora and the fauna of the area. Bradford had a strong sense of appreciation of the environment in which he moved, and we are grateful to him for this account of the early natural history of southeastern Massachusetts.

Then followed a series of four journeys described by Edward Winslow, who participated in them. The first was a trip to Massasoit in 1621 by Winslow and Stephen Hopkins. Again we are treated to an excellent description of the land to the southwest of Plymouth. We also obtain a picture of the relationship between Massasoit and the Pilgrims, Indian life and attitudes, Indian homes, Indian food, and Indian generosity.

Like Bradford, Winslow was observant. Writing of an area near my home, he stated:

> As we passed along, we observed that there were few places by the river, but had been inhabited by reason whereof, much ground was clear, save of weeds which grew higher than our heads. There is much good timber both oak, walnut tree, fir, beech, and exceeding great chestnut trees. The country in respect to the lying of it is both champaign and hilly, like many places in England. In some places it's very rocky both above ground and in it. And though the country be wild and overgrown with woods, yet the trees stand not thick, but a man may well ride a horse amongst them.

MOURT'S
RELATION:
A JOURNAL
OF THE
PILGRIMS OF
PLYMOUTH

A HISTORY OF
MOURT'S
RELATION

In the summer of 1621 John Billington, a young boy, was lost on Cape Cod, and some men went to the Cape to find him. Winslow wrote an account of this trip and through this relation we meet some interesting Indians, with whom the Pilgrims had interesting relationships in the next few years. Winslow looked around, and saw much, and recorded the events and described the country in detail. On a short trip from Nauset (Eastham) to Cummaquid he noted that:

the soil at Nauset and here is alike, even and sandy, not so good for corn as where we are. Ships may ride safely in either harbor . . .

Two more trips were described in detail, one to Nemasket and a trip to its Massachusetts tribe in Boston Bay. In the former we become aware that the English were able to impose their will on the Indians by sheer strength of superior weapons. In the account of the visit to the Massachusetts we read a good description of Boston Bay, the fishing areas, and the mouths of the Charles and Mystic rivers. The Indians feared the English at first, but they finally realized that the English had come only for trade. Squanto, who accompanied them, suggested that they take the "skins, and all such things as might be serviceable for us," explaining that they were a bad people, and would certainly have dealt badly with the English if they dared. Winslow's reply was a combination of lofty and noble language and thorough pragmatism. He said:

Were they ever so bad we would not wrong them or give them any just occasion against us; for their words we little weighed them, but if they once attempted any thing against us, then we would deal far worse than he desired.

The pamphlet also contained a letter signed "E. W.," obviously Edward Winslow, to a friend in England, undoubtedly George Morton, containing Bradford's earlier account from the spring to the fall of 1621. There was nothing spectacular in the report, but the letter was a glowing account of a successful plantation.

The letter contained the first printed account of the Pilgrim's Thanksgiving dinner. Winslow told how they had planted twelve acres of Indian corn and fertilized it with herring, "which we have in great abundance and take with great ease at our doors."

In all honesty, Winslow admitted that not all farming was successful. He wrote:

Our corn did prove well and God be praised; we had a good increase of Indian corn, and our barley indifferent good, but our peas not worth the gathering, for we feared they came up very well, and blossomed, but the sun parched them in the blossoms.

Finally Winslow wrote:

Our harvest having been gotten in, our Governor sent four fowling that so we might after a more special manner rejoice together, after we had gathered the fruit of our labors. They four in one day killed as much food as with a little help beside served the company almost a week at which time amongst other recreations, we exercised our arms, many of the Indians coming amongst us, and among the rest their greatest king, Massasoit, with some ninety men, whom for three days we entertained and feasted, and they went out and killed five deer, which they brought to the Plantation and bestowed on our Governor and upon the Captain and others.

Again, there in a touch of anthropology and sociology, Winslow explained that the Indians remained friendly, for, he wrote that "it hath pleased God to possess the Indians with a fear of us and love unto us." He also pointed out that the relations between the Indians and English had brought "great peace among the Indians themselves" and that:

> We for our part walk as peaceably and safely in the woods as in the highways in England; we entertain them in our houses, and they as friendly bestow venison on us.

He described the Indians further as:

> a people without any religion or knowledge of God, yet very trusting, quick of apprehension, ripe witted, just.

The food in Plymouth was good and plentiful. Fish and fowl were available in abundance, and the bay was

> full of lobsters all the summer, and affordeth us a variety of other fish; in September we can take a hogshead of eels in a night, with small labor and can dig them out of their beds.
> There were salad herbs, "grapes white and red and very sweet and strong also," and there were strawberries, raspberries, and plums as well.

There was a purpose in Winslow's letter. Plymouth needed men and women who were ready to settle there and to develop the new plantation. The remainder of Winslow's letter was a strong treatise for the prospective settler. Bring a strong bread-box, he asserted, "to put your biscuits in," and an iron-board cask for beer and water. Bring some meal to last until you can get a crop in, and some salted meat, for there were no cattle in the colony at that time. The settlers were advised to bring a fowling piece, lemon juice, butter or salad oil, paper and linseed oil for windows, cotton yarn for lamps, powder and shot. He warned the settlers not to waste space by bringing rice for "our Indian corn, even the coarsest, maketh as pleasant a meat as rice."

We boast today about "making it in Massachusetts." Obviously, according to his account, the Pilgrims were making it in Plymouth. What effect the letter had in inducing people to move to Plymouth is not known. George Morton, to whom the letter was written, migrated to Plymouth the following year.

The final essay in the book was written by Robert Cushman and entitled "Reasons and Consideration Touching the Lawfulness of Removing out of England into the Parts of America." It is of little historical importance. Cushman tried to point out that there was no Scriptural objection to a person settling a new colony away from home. Heath described it well and simply as "a thinly veiled promotional

MOURT'S
RELATION:
A JOURNAL
OF THE
PILGRIMS OF
PLYMOUTH

A HISTORY OF
MOURT'S
RELATION

tract organized like a sermon, which cites Scripture to justify the plantation and to persuade others to follow."

The printing and publishing history of *Mourt's Relation,* as the pamphlet is popularly called, is an especially fascinating exercise in biobibliography. The name *Mourt's Relation* was a short name given to identify the work in Prince's *Annals* and the name has stayed with the book for almost 250 years.

The pamphlet had been in print a short time when John Smith planned to write an account of the Pilgrim settlement at Plymouth. He used *Mourt's Relation* extensively in preparing his History of Virginia, New England and the Summer Isles published in London in 1624.

In 1625 Samuel Purchas, who was preparing his famous *Pilgrims,* abridged *Mourt's Relation* and included it in his fifth volume, so that it was once again widely disseminated.

Almost every historian of New England from 1669, when Nathaniel Morton's *New England Memorial* appeared, used this book. The Rev. Thomas Prince, the teacher of the Old South Church, used it extensively in preparing the *Annals,* and, as I have observed, gave it its abbreviated name. Purchas's condensed version was printed in the Massachusetts Historical Society Collection (pp. 203-239) in 1802. Twenty years later the work was reprinted in the Collections but many sections were missing, and the work was scattered over several volumes, so that for scholarly purposes, it was a disaster.

Then in 1841 Alexander Young published his valuable *Chronicle of the Pilgrim Fathers* of the Colony of Plymouth from 1602 to 1625. Young, pastor of the New South Church in Boston, had a love for the Pilgrims and showed it in his treatment of the original accounts. They were translated into nineteenth century English, the spelling and punctuation were changed, and so the newly published account became easy to read. In addition Dr. Young provided copious footnotes and excellent annotations, for which all students of the Pilgrim Fathers since his time must be eternally grateful.

A few years later Dr. George B. Cheever, a Congregational clergyman and a well-known nineteenth century reformer, prepared a volume called *The Journal of the Pilgrims at Plymouth, in New England, in 1620. Reprinted from the Original Volume with Historical and Local Illustrations of Providences, Principles, and Prisms.* This book, which was published in New York in 1848, contained a reprint of *Mourt's Relation,* with the spelling and punctuation unchanged but in 19th century typography. In addition, Cheever added many chapters detailing the history and religious philosophy of the Founding Fathers. Despite the fact that it was written about 135 years ago, the book reveals the author's excellent understanding of the Pilgrims. Particularly, it must be remembered that this book was written several years before the rediscovery of Bradford's manuscript of *Of Plimoth Plantation.* The volume went through several printings between 1848 and the Civil War including one in Glasgow.

In 1865 Henry Martyn Dexter, a Congregationalist editor, and a direct descendant of George Morton, prepared a new edition of *Mourt's Relation.* Limited to 285 copies this volume was issued in J. K. Wiggin's Library of New England History; this work is invaluable.

Dr. Dexter used the copious notes prepared by Dr. Alexander Young in 1841, for which he gave him full credit, and added a great many of his own. This volume contained excellent detailed maps so it is of great use to the modern scholar. It was not a facsimile edition, but the author did retain the original spelling, punctuation and paragraphing and reproduced the 17th century type as well. Unfortunately this makes the book difficult to read, but its notes give this edition its great value.

Shortly before the turn of the century Edward Arber, the British historian who had a deep interest in the Pilgrims, edited a work called *The Story of the Pilgrim Fathers,* which included many original works. *Mourt's Relation* was one of those selected and appeared on pages 395-505.

By the end of World War I tourists to this part of the country were interested in reading about some of the places to which they had travelled. A Cape Cod gift shop owner took advantage of this interest by extracting those portions of *Mourt's Relation* which dealt with Cape Cod and prepared a pamphlet called *The Cape Cod Journal of the Pilgrim Fathers.* This pamphlet had an introduction and notes by Lyon Sherman and a cover design by John C. Pratt. This little pamphlet remained in print for many years.

One of the loveliest editions of *Mourt's Relation,* which no amount of advertising in the country and in Great Britain has resulted in someone being willing to sell his copy, was published in London in 1939 under the title *The Pilgrim Fathers, a Journal of Their Coming in the Mayflower to New England and Their Life and Adventures There.* The book was edited with an introduction, preface, and notes by the world-famous bibliographer Theodore Besterman. It was illustrated with eight engravings by Geoffrey Wales. This edition was limited to 300 numbered copies and printed by the famous Golden Cockerell Press.

In that same year (1939), a new reprint entitled *Homes in the Wilderness, a Pilgrims Journal of Plymouth Plantation in 1620,* was published in New York. The authors' names were given as "William Bradford and Others of the Mayflower Company," and the book contained a very short introduction but no notes.

Dwight B. Heath, then a professor at Brown University, was the editor of a reprint which appeared in 1963 called *A Journal of the Pilgrims at Plymouth.* The book, in which the paragraphing, spelling, punctuation and typography were modernized, contains few notes but there is a brilliant short introduction, and the book contains many photographs taken at Plimoth Plantation.

In 1966 University Microprint of the University of Michigan in Ann Arbor reprinted the work in excellent facsimile, good and clear and black, so it is possible for scholars to study the original printing. This work has recently been rebound by Barnes and Noble in their *Great Americans* Series and has been available at discount prices. Another facsimile edition was produced by the Pequot Library at Southport, Connecticut, in 1967.

Recently Mr. Lawrence D. Pizer, Director of the Pilgrim Society, brought to my attention a reprint produced by Preston Limited in Bolton, Lancashire, England in 1970. This edition contains an excellent short introduction by Michael Marshall. It is a limited edition; 2050 copies were printed in brown ink on Cream Antique Laid paper. The spelling is uncorrected, but the punctuation and paragraphing are much improved. Nicely bound in board, it is an excellent example of modern artistic bookmaking.

My own edition of *Mourt's Relation* is the result of a careful reading of the original edition and the other editions and printings that have been prepared. I, too, have corrected spelling and punctuation, have done some reparagraphing, and have tried to correct some errors that older editions have not noted.

MOURT'S
RELATION:
A JOURNAL
OF THE
PILGRIMS OF
PLYMOUTH

A HISTORY OF
MOURT'S
RELATION

My edition is heavily annotated. Indeed the text contains about 100 double-spaced typewritten sheets and the section on notes and documentation is at least as long. As Dexter has used Young's notes and Young has used Freeman's, I have used the best of their notes and have added many of my own. I have traveled over almost all of the territory mentioned in the original pamphlet, much of it by foot and some of it by boat. Needless to say the area is much changed, but with a little imagination, and historians certainly possess that attribute, it is not difficult to reconstruct in the mind's eye the land as it once was.

More than 100 years ago when Dexter, and Young, and Freeman wrote and researched, there were few real scholars of the Pilgrim story. Today's editor is more fortunate. The Plymouth Rock Foundation, of which Mr. John G. Talcott, Jr., who was formerly president of the Pilgrim Society, serves as president, has supported and encouraged this research. I had also the privilege of discussing my procedure with Dr. Peter Gomes, secretary of the Pilgrim Society, and the late Dr. Walter Muir Whitehill, who among others was also a Pilgrim Fellow, as is Dr. Gomes. Three other Pilgrim Fellows read the edition and made pertinent comments and suggestions. They were Dr. Harry Ward of the University of Richmond, Dr. George Horner, professor emeritus of Anthropology at Boston University and Bridgewater State College, and Miss Rose Briggs, who for many years was the mainstay of the Society and its Collections.

Mourt's Relation is excellent first-hand history, an invaluable primary source for Pilgrim history. With some allowances made for the exaggeration and color in Winslow's account, which we know was necessary to induce others to come here, the account is still excellent first-hand history. Winslow was certainly the patron saint of several generations of realtors, public relations experts and tourists and travel agents who followed him and his examples.

But it is more than a simple historical account. It is outstanding documentary drama. Just as an account of a great adventure it makes exciting reading. One of the reasons that I corrected spelling, punctuation, and other items was so that the general reader might enjoy it as a fascinating narrative.

The pamphlet gives us a key to the land around Plymouth 360 years ago and presents a good narrative of historical events that might not otherwise have been known. Most of all it gives us a good portrait of the Pilgrim Fathers, that hardy, unassuming people who came to this area, settled and developed it, and remain an emblem of right and virtue to us to this day. Others came before them, and many others have come since, but we can certainly say with Goldwin Smith, "Columbus discovered a new land, but the Pilgrims discovered a new world."

Bridgewater, Massachusetts   Jordan D. Fiore
March, 1985

A
RELATION OR

Iournall of the beginning and proceedings
of the English Plantation setled at *Plimoth* in NEW
ENGLAND, by certaine English Aduenturers both
Merchants and others.

With their difficult passage, their safe ariuall, their
ioyfull building of, and comfortable planting them-
selues in the now well defended Towne
of NEW PLIMOTH.

AS ALSO A RELATION OF FOVRE
seuerall discoueries since made by some of the
same English Planters there resident.

I. In a iourney to PVCKANOKICK the habitation of the Indians greatest King Massasoyt : as also their message, the answer and entertainment
they had of him.

II. In a voyage made by ten of them to the Kingdome of Nawset, to seeke
a boy that had lost himselfe in the woods : with such accidents as befell them
in that voyage.

III. In their iourney to the Kingdome of Namaschet, in defence of their
greatest King Massasoyt, against the Narrohigronsets, and to reuenge the
supposed death of their Interpreter Tisquantum.

IIII. Their voyage to the Massachusets, and their entertainment there.

With an answer to all such obiections as are any way made
against the lawfulnesse of English plantations
in those parts.

LONDON,
Printed for *Iohn Bellamie*, and are to be sold at his shop at the two
Greyhounds in Cornhill neere the Royall Exchange. 1622.

Title Page of 1622 Edition of *Mourt's Relation*

TO HIS MUCH RESPECTED FRIEND, MR. I. P.[1]

Good Friend,

As we cannot but account it an extraordinary blessing of God in directing our course for these parts, after we came out of our native country, — for that we had the happiness to be possessed of the comforts we receive by the benefit of one of the most pleasant, most healthful, and most fruitful parts of the world, — so must we acknowledge the same blessing to be multiplied upon our whole company, for that we obtained the honor to receive allowance and approbation of our free possession and enjoying thereof, under the authority of those thrice honored persons, The President and Council for the Affairs of New England;[2] by whose bounty and grace, in that behalf, all of us are tied to dedicate our best service unto them, as those, under his Majesty, that we owe it unto; whose noble endeavours in these their actions the God of heaven and earth multiply to his glory and their own eternal comforts.

As for this poor *Relation,* I pray you to accept it as being writ by the several actors themselves,[3] after their plain and rude manner. Therefore, doubt nothing of the truth thereof. If it be defective in any thing, it is their ignorance, that are better acquainted with planting than writing. If it satisfy those that are well affected to the business, it is all I care for. Sure I am the place we are in, and the hopes that are ap-

---

1. I. P. undoubtedly "stands for John Peirce, Citizen and Clothworker of London, who had interested himself to assist the Leyden men in coming over, and in whose name their first Patent was taken." (Dexter, p. xxxv)

2. Young explains (p. 114), "The Pilgrims by coming so far north, had got beyond the limits of the Virginia Company, and accordingly their patent was of no value. On the return of the *Mayflower* in May, 1621, the Merchant adventurers applied, in their behalf, to the President and Council of New England, for a grant of the territory on which they had unintentionally settled. This it seems was readily accorded."

3. According to Young (p. 115), "This constitutes its great value, and confers on it the highest authority." Note that George Morton ("G. Mourt") in "To the Reader" that follows this section states that these relations came "to my hands from my both known and faithful friends, on whose writings I do much rely." Young does not "hesitate to ascribe this Journal to Bradford and Winslow, chiefly to the former. They were among the most active and efficient leaders of the Pilgrims; and one or the other of them went on almost every expedition here recorded, and were therefore cognizant to the facts as eye-witnesses." Young admits that others might have provided information for this journal, but "the part they contributed to it, if any, would probably be confined to furnishing the rough sketches of such expeditions as those to Nauset, Namaschet, and Massachusetts, in which Bradford and Winslow may not have been personally engaged. The style, too, seems to correspond, in its plainness and directness, with that of Bradford, in his History."

MOURT'S
RELATION:
A JOURNAL
OF THE
PILGRIMS OF
PLYMOUTH

parent, cannot but suffice any that will not desire more than enough. Neither is there want of aught among us but company to enjoy the blessing so plentifully bestowed upon the inhabitants that are here. While I was writing this, I had almost forgot that I had but the recommendation of the Relation itself to your further consideration, and therefore I will end without saying more, save that I shall always rest,

Yours, in the way of friendship,

R. G.[4]

From Plymouth, in New England

---

4. *R. G.* is undoubtedly a misprint for R. C. or Robert Cushman. He came to Plymouth on the *Fortune* in November, 1621, and returned to England in December, 1621. Cushman brought the information that a patent had been obtained for them by the merchants of London from the President and Council of New England "better than the former, and with less limitation." He probably carried the journal and the additions to England for publication.

Pilgrim Rock on Clark's Island in Plymouth Harbor, Site of the First
Religious Service in the New World. *Courtesy of the Pilgrim Society*

TO THE READER

Courteous Reader,

Be entreated to make a favorable construction of my forwardness in publishing these ensuing discourses. The desire of carrying the Gospel of Christ into those foreign parts, amongst those people that as yet have had no knowledge nor taste of God, as also to procure unto themselves and others a quiet and comfortable habitation, were, amongst other things, the inducements unto these undertakers of the then hopeful, and now experimentally known good enterprise for plantation in New England, to set afoot and prosecute the same. And though it fared with them, as it is common to the most actions of this nature, that the first attempts prove difficult, as the sequel more at large expresseth, yet it hath pleased God, even beyond our expectation in so short a time, to give hope of letting some of them see (though some he hath taken out of this vale of tears)[1] some grounds of hope of the accomplishment of both those ends by them at first propounded.

And as myself then much desire, and shortly hope to effect, if the Lord will, the putting to of my shoulder in this hopeful business, and in the meantime these Relations coming to my hand from my both known and faithful friends, on whose writings I do much rely, I thought it not amiss to make them more general, hoping of a cheerful proceeding both of adventurers and planters; entreating that the example of the honorable Virginia and Bermudas[2] Companies, encountering with so many disasters, and that for divers years together with an unwearied resolution, the good effects whereof are now eminent, may prevail as a spur of preparation also touching this no less hopeful[3] country, though yet an infant, the extent and commodities whereof are as yet not fully known: after time will unfold more. Such as desire to take knowledge of things, may inform themselves by this ensuing treatise, and, if

---

1. Young (p. III) notes that, "The writer studiously suppresses the discouraging fact that more than *half* of the first Colonists had already perished." It is true that Bradford, who undoubtedly wrote the first portion of this journal, does not detail the deaths of that first winter. Dr. Thomas Prince, who used Bradford's original work that was subsequently first published (1856) as *Of Plimoth Plantation* in preparing his *New England Chronology* refers to a notebook of Bradford's that gave the actual dates of the deaths of many passengers. This notebook has evidently been lost.

2. The Bermudas and all islands three hundred leagues from the coast were within the jurisdiction of the Virginia Company in the third patent granted in 1612. The Company sold these islands to 120 of their own members who formed a new and separate corporation under the title of the Simer Islands Company.

3. Despite John Smith's favorable description of New England in 1616, most persons, recalling the failure of Popham's colony at Sagadahoc in 1608, regarded New England as "a cold, barren, mountainous, rocky desert. . . . uninhabitable by Englishmen."

MOURT'S
RELATION:
A JOURNAL
OF THE
PILGRIMS OF
PLYMOUTH

TO THE
READER

they please also by such as have been there a first and second time.[4] My hearty prayer to God is that the event of his and all other honorable and honest undertakings may be for the furtherance of the kingdom of Christ, the enlarging of the bounds of our sovereign lord, King James, and the good and profit of those who, either by purse or person or both, are agents in the same. So I take leave, and rest

Thy friend,

G. Mourt.[5]

---

4. Young (p. 112) notes that "Cushman had just returned from Plymouth, and Clark and Coppin, the mates or pilots of the *Mayflower,* had been on the coast twice."

5. Both Dexter and Young agree that "G. Mourt" was most likely George Morton, a member of this colony at Leyden who was in London at this time. Young (p. 113) erroneously identifies George Morton as a man "who had married a sister of Gov. Bradford." Morton's wife was Juliana Carpenter, whose sister, Alice Carpenter Southworth, was Bradford's second wife. Morton and his wife came to Plymouth in the *Anne* in July, 1623, bringing with them their five children. George Morton died a year later, and Bradford raised Morton's eldest son, Nathaniel, who was then eleven years old. To Nathaniel, who was secretary of the colony for many years, we are indebted for the preservation of one of Bradford's Dialogues, the Plymouth Church Records, and his book published in 1669, *New Englands Memoriall.*

Statue of William Bradford, Near Plymouth Rock
Courtesy of the Pilgrim Society

CERTAIN USEFUL ADVERTISEMENTS SENT IN A LETTER WRITTEN BY A DISCREET FRIEND[1] UNTO THE PLANTERS IN NEW ENGLAND, AT THEIR FIRST SETTING SAIL FROM SOUTHAMPTON, WHO ERNESTLY DESIRETH THE PROSPERITY OF THAT THEIR NEW PLANTATION

Loving and Christian friends,

I do heartily and in the Lord salute you all, as being they with whom I am present in my best affection and most earnest longings after you, though I be constrained for a while to be bodily absent from you.[2] I say constrained, God knowing how willingly and much rather than otherwise I would have borne my part with you in this first brunt, were I not by strong necessity held back for the present. Make account of me in the meanwhile as of a man divided in myself in great pain, and as (natural bonds set aside) having my better part with you. And though I doubt not but in your godly wisdoms you both foresee and resolve upon that which concerneth your present state and condition both severally and jointly, yet have I thought[3] but my duty to add some further spur of provocation unto them who run already, if not because you need it, yet because I owe it in love and duty.

---

1. This letter from John Robinson, written in July, 1620, has been reprinted frequently. In addition to its inclusion in this publication, it was copied into Bradford's account (Of Plimoth Plantation) and in Nathaniel Morton's *New Englands Memoriall* (1669), pages 6-9.

2. The original printing has a comma at this point, Bradford's has a period, and Morton has a colon.

3. Bradford and Morton both add *it*. The comparisons between the original text and the accounts by Bradford and Morton are taken from Dexter's edition of the *Relation*.

MOURT'S
RELATION:
A JOURNAL
OF THE
PILGRIMS OF
PLYMOUTH

CERTAIN USEFUL
ADVERTISEMENTS
SENT IN A LET-
TER WRITTEN
BY A DISCREET
FRIEND UNTO
THE PLANTERS
IN NEW ENG-
LAND, AT THEIR
FIRST SETTING
SAIL FROM
SOUTHAMPTON,
WHO ERNESTLY
DESIRETH THE
PROSPERITY OF
THAT THEIR
NEW PLANTATION

And first, as we are daily to renew our repentance with our God, special[4] for our sins known, and general for our[5] unknown trespasses; so doth the Lord call us in a singular manner, upon occasions of such difficulty and danger as lieth upon you, to a both more narrow search and careful reformation of our ways in His sight, lest He calling to remembrance our sins forgotten by us or unrepented of, take advantage against us, and in judgement leave us for the same to be swallowed up in one danger or other. Whereas, on the contrary, sin being taken away by earnest repentance, and the pardon thereof from the Lord sealed up unto a man's conscience by his Spirit, great shall be his security and peace in all dangers, sweet his comforts in all distresses, with happy deliverance from all evil, whether in life or in death.

Now next after this heavenly peace with God and our own consciences, we are carefully to provide for peace with all men what in us lieth, especially with our associates, and for that end[6] watchfulness must be had, that we neither at all in our selves do give, no nor easily take offense being, given by others. Woe be unto the world for offenses, for though it be necessary (considering the malice of Satan and man's corruption) that offenses come, yet woe unto the man or woman either by whom the offense cometh, saith Christ. (Matthew xviii, 7) And if offenses in the unseasonable use of things in themselves indifferent, be more to be feared than death itself, as the Apostle teacheth (I Corinthians ix, 15) how much more in things simply evil, in which neither honor of God nor love of man is thought worthy to be regarded.

Neither yet is it sufficient that we keep ourselves by the grace of God from giving offense, except withal we be armed against the taking of them when they are[7] given by others.[8] For how unperfect and lame is the work of grace in that person, who want charity to cover a multitude of offenses,[9] as the Scriptures speak. Neither are you to be exhorted to this grace only upon the common grounds of Christianity, which are, that persons ready to take offense either want charity to cover offenses[9] or wisdom duly to weigh human frailty, or lastly are gross, though close hypocrites, as Christ our Lord teacheth, (Matthew vii, 1-5) as indeed in mine own experience, few or none have been found which sooner give offense, them such as easily take it; neither have they ever proved sound and profitable members in societies, which have nourished in themselves that touchy humor.[10] But besides these there are divers special[11] motives provoking you above others to great care and conscience this way: As first, you are many of you strangers as to the persons, so to the infirmities one of another, and so stand in need of more watchfulness this way, lest when such things fall out in men and women as you suspected not, you be inordinately affected with them; which doth require at your hands much wisdom and charity for the covering and preventing of incident offenses that way. And lastly, your intended course of

---

4. Bradford and Morton read *especially*.

5. Bradford and Morton both use *your* instead of *our*.

6. Bradford and Morton omit *end*.

7. Bradford has *be*.

8. Morton has a colon here.

9. Young notes (p. 93) that the passage between the *offenses* in this paragraph is omitted in the copy Morton made for the Plymouth Church records, obviously an accidental omission since the passage is included in his *New Englands Memoriall* (1669).

10. Bradford reads, "which have nourished this touchy humor;" Morton reads, "who had nourished this touchy humor."

11. Bradford and Morton both omit *special*.

civil community[12] will minister continual occasion of offense, and will be as full for that fire, except you diligently quench it with brotherly forbearance. And if taking of offense causelessly or easily at men's doings be so carefully to be avoided, how much more heed is to be taken that we take not offense at God himself, which yet we certainly do so oft[13] as we do murmur as His providence in our crosses or bear impatiently such afflictions as wherewith He pleaseth to visit us. Store we up[14] therefore patience against the evil day, without which we take offense at the Lord Himself in His holy and just works.

A fourth thing there is carefully to be provided for, to wit, that with your common employments you join common affections truly bent upon the general good, avoiding as a deadly plague of your both common and special comfort all retiredness of mind for proper advantage, and all singularly affected any manner of way; let every man repress in himself and the whole body in each person, as so many rebels against the common good, all private respects of men's selves, not sorting with the general convenience. And as men are careful not to have a new house shaken with any violence before it be well settled and the parts firmly knit,[15] so be you, I beseech you brethren, much more careful that the house of God which you are, and are to be, be not shaken with unnecessary novelties or other oppositions at the first settling thereof.

Lastly, whereas you are to[16] become a body politic, using amongst yourselves civil government, and are not furnished with any persons of special eminence above the rest, to be chosen by you into office of government.[17] Let your wisdom and godliness appear, not only in choosing such persons as do entirely love, and will diligently promote the common good,[18] but also in yielding unto them all due honor and obedience in their lawful administrations; not beholding in them the ordinariness of their persons, but God's ordinance for your good; nor being like unto the foolish multitude,[19] who more honor the gay coat, than either the virtuous mind of the man, or glorious ordinance of the Lord. But you know better things, and that the image of the Lord's power and authority, which the magistrate beareth, is honorable, in how mean persons soever. And this duty you both may the more willingly, and ought the more conscionably to perform, because you are at least for the present to have only them for your ordinary governors, which yourselves shall make choice of for that work.[20]

Sundry other things of importance I could put you in mind of, and of those before mentioned in more words, but I will not so far wrong your godly minds, as to think you heedless of these things, there being also divers among you so well able to

MOURT'S RELATION: A JOURNAL OF THE PILGRIMS OF PLYMOUTH

CERTAIN USEFUL ADVERTISEMENTS SENT IN A LETTER WRITTEN BY A DISCREET FRIEND UNTO THE PLANTERS IN NEW ENGLAND, AT THEIR FIRST SETTING SAIL FROM SOUTHAMPTON, WHO ERNESTLY DESIRETH THE PROSPERITY OF THAT THEIR NEW PLANTATION

---

12. Dexter (p. xliv) notes, "I cannot interpret this otherwise than as an intimation that the Pilgrims left Holland with the full intention of establishing here a popular civil government; with the good will, if not the prompting, of their noble pastor. And the 'lastly' clause of this letter confirms this view."

13. Bradford has *ofte* (often).

14. Bradford and Morton both omit *we*.

15. Bradford has a comma.

16. Bradford omits *to*.

17. Bradford has a comma; Morton a semicolon.

18. Bradford has a comma, Morton a colon.

19. Bradford and Morton both read "not being like the foolish multitude."

20. John Carver was evidently chosen governor before they left, confirmed after the Mayflower Compact was signed, and reelected in March, 1621.

MOURT'S
RELATION:
A JOURNAL
OF THE
PILGRIMS OF
PLYMOUTH

CERTAIN USEFUL
ADVERTISEMENTS
SENT IN A LET-
TER WRITTEN
BY A DISCREET
FRIEND UNTO
THE PLANTERS
IN NEW ENG-
LAND, AT THEIR
FIRST SETTING
SAIL FROM
SOUTHAMPTON,
WHO ERNESTLY
DESIRETH THE
PROSPERITY OF
THAT THEIR
NEW PLANTATION

admonish both themselves and others of what concerneth them. These few things, therefore, and the same in few words, I do earnestly commend unto your care and conscience, joining therewith my daily incessant prayers unto the Lord, that He who hath made the heavens and the earth, the sea and all rivers of waters, and whose providence is over all His works, especially over all His dear children for good, would so guide and guard you in your ways, as inwardly by His spirit, so outwardly by the hand of His power, as that both you and we also, for and with you, may have after praising his name all the days of your and our lives. Fare you well in Him in whom you trust, and in whom I rest

> An unfeigned well-willed of
> your happy success in this
> hopeful voyage,
>
> I. R.[21]

---

21. This letter is undated, but John Robinson wrote to John Carver on July 27, 1620, "I have written a large letter to the whole, and am sorry I shall not rather speak than write to them."

In ye name of God Amen. We whose names are underwriten,
the loyall subjects of our dread soveraigne Lord King James
by ye grace of God, of great Britaine, franc, & Ireland king
defender of ye faith, &c

Haueing undertaken, for ye glorie of God, and aduancemente
of ye christian faith and honour of our king & countrie, a voyage to
plant ye first colonie in ye Northerne parts of Virginia. Doe
by these presents solemnly & mutualy in ye presence of God, and
one of another, couenant, & combine our selues togeather into a
ciuill body politick; for our better ordering, & preseruation & fur=
therance of ye ends aforesaid; and by vertue hearof to enacte,
constitute, and frame shuch just & equall lawes, ordinances,
Acts, constitutions, & offices, from time to time, as shall be thought
most meete & conuenient for ye generall good of ye colonie: unto
which we promise all due submission and obedience. In witnes
wherof we haue hereunder subscribed our names at Cap=
Codd ye ·11· of Nouember, in ye year of ye raigne of our soueraigne
Lord King James of England, franc, & Ireland ye eighteenth
and of Scotland ye fiftie fourth. Ano: Dom. 1620.

Bradford's Account of the *Mayflower Compact*,
from His Manuscript of *Of Plimoth Plantation*
in Massachusetts State Archives, Boston

A Relation or Journal of the Proceedings of the Plantation Settled at Plymouth in New England

(I)

WEDNESDAY, the sixth of September.[1] The wind coming east-north-east,[2] a fine small gale, we loosed from Plymouth, having been kindly entertained and courteously used by divers friends there dwelling; and after many difficulties in boisterous storms, at length, by God's providence, upon the ninth of November[3] following, by break of the day, we espied land, which we deemed to be Cape Cod, and so afterward it proved. And the appearance of it much comforted us, especially seeing so goodly a land, and wooded to the brink of the sea.[4] It caused us to rejoice together, and praise God that had given us once again to see land. And thus we made our course south-south-west,[5] purposing to go to a river[6] ten leagues to the south of the Cape.[7] But at night the wind being contrary,[8] we put round again for the

---

1. New style—September 16, 1620.

2. Dexter notes, *"East-north-east* was the fairest possible wind for leaving Plymouth, as the direct course down the Sound to the Channel and thence toward the open sea, would not be far from s.w. by s. and w.s.s." (p. 1)

3. Thursday, November 19, 1620.

4. Dexter states that at the time of the Pilgrims' arrival, the Cape Cod area could boast of "a comely if not luxuriant growth of trees and forest vegetation." (p. 2)

5. According to Bradford, "they backed about and resolved to stand for the southward (the wind and weather being fair) to find some place about Hudson's river for their habitation." Dexter reasons, "Even with the greatest possible offing when they made land, they could hardly have steered long in a s.s.w. course, as it would have brought them directly on the cape. An error of the press for south-south-east is not improbable." (p. 2)

6. Hudson River. Young believes that *ten* leagues probably is a printer's error. (p. 117)

7. "Their ideas of the relative positions of most points on the New England shore were then of the vaguest." (Dexter, p. 2)

8. Bradford recalled that "After they had sailed the course about half the day, they fell amongst dangerous shoals and roaring breakers, and they were so far entangled therewith as they concerned themselves in great danger; and the wind shrinking upon them withal, they resolved to bear up again for the Cape, and thought themselves happy to get out of those dangers before night overtook them, as by God's Providence they did." The consensus of several experts is that the shoals were probably located then off Eastham and Orleans.

MOURT'S
RELATION:
A JOURNAL
OF THE
PILGRIMS OF
PLYMOUTH

A RELATION OR
JOURNAL OF THE
PROCEEDINGS OF
THE PLANTATION
SETTLED AT
PLYMOUTH IN
NEW ENGLAND

bay of Cape Cod; and upon the 11th of November[9] we came to an anchor in the bay,[10] which is a good harbor and pleasant bay,[11] circled round,[12] except in the entrance, which is about four miles over from land to land,[13] compassed about to the very sea with oaks, pines, juniper, sassafras, and other sweet wood.[14] It is a harbor wherein a thousand sail of ships may safely ride.[15] There we relieved ourselves with wood and water, and refreshed our people, while our shallop was fitted to coast the bay, to search for a habitation. There was the greatest store of fowl[16] that ever we saw.

And every day we saw whales[17] playing hard by us; of which in that place, if we had instruments and means to take them, we might have made a very rich return; which, to our great grief, we wanted. Our master and his mate, and others experienced in fishing, professed we might have made three or four thousand pounds' worth of oil. They preferred it before Greenland whale-fishing, and purpose the next

---

9. Saturday, November 21, 1620. (n.s.)

10. Provincetown harbor.

11. According to Young, Cape Cod harbor "is formed by the spiral bending of the land, from Pamet river to Long Point, nearly round every point of the compass; it is completely land-locked." He quotes from a report by Major J. D. Graham published as No. 121 of *Executive Documents of the 25th Congress.* 2d session, 1837-8, volume 5. Graham writes of the harbor, "It is one of the finest harbors for ships of war on the whole of our Atlantic Coast. The width, and freedom from obstructions of every kind, at its entrance, and the extent of searoom upon the bay side, make it accessible to vessels of the largest class in almost all winds. This advantage, its capacity, depth of water, excellent anchorage, and the complete shelter it affords from all winds, render it one of the most valuable ship harbors upon our coast, whether considered in a commercial or military point of view."

12. The harbor is in the form of a broken circle.

13. "This is just the distance from long Point to the nearest land in Truro," Young writes. (p. 118) Dexter adds, "As the inner shore of the cape trends away s.e. by s., the distance across the entrance varies, according to the angle at which it was taken, from 2½ miles, which is the nearest line from Long Point light to the Eastharbor there, to 5½ miles; from the same light to the opening of Pamet River, in Truro." (p. 3)

14. In 1841 Young noted, "Few trees are now left round Cape Cod harbor. That they were once common, appears from the name *Wood End,* given to a part of the coast, and from the stumps that are still found along the shore, particularly at the west end of the harbor, below the present high water mark, just above what is called 'the rising.' There is quite a grove of pines, called Mayo's Wood, near Snow's Hill, at the eastern end of the village. There are dwarf oaks, too, growing on High Hill. The young trees would thrive if they were enclosed and protected from the cows, who now get part of their living by browsing on them. There are a few sassafras bushes, but no juniper. The juniper was probably the red cedar. Josselyn in his *New England's Rarities,* published in 1672, says, page 49, 'Carden says juniper is cedar in hot countries and juniper in cold countries; it is here very dwarfish and shrubby, growing for the most part by the seaside.' And Wood, in his *New England's Prospect,* printed in 1634, says, p. 19, 'the cedar tree is a tree of no great growth, not bearing above a foot and a half at the most, neither is it very high. The wood is of color red and white, like yew, smelling as sweet as juniper.' In 1740 there was a number of oaks in the woods northwest of East Harbor." (p. 118)

15. The changes of more than 350 years have not abridged this capacity. More than a century ago Freeman wrote in his *History of Cape Cod,* II, 619, that "the harbor is sufficiently capacious for 3,000 vessels, and is a haven of the greatest importance to navigation, whether as respects vessels doing business in the neighboring waters, or ships from foreign voyages arriving on the coast in thick and stormy weather."

16. Young notes (p. 119) that "Sea fowl come late in the autumn and remain during the winter. . . ." Dexter adds (p. 2) that "Sea-fowl are plenty on the shores and in the bay; particularly the gannet, curlew, brant, black-duck, sea-duck, old wife, dipper, sheldrake, penguins, gull, plover, coot, widgeon, and peep."

17. According to Young (p. 119), writing in 1841, "Whales are frequently seen in Barnstable Bay and on the outside of the Cape, and are killed by boats from Provincetown. Occasionally, though more rarely of late, they come into the harbor; at the beginning of the present century, two or three whales, producing about a hundred barrels of oil, were annually caught . . ." Freeman (*History of Cape Cod,* II, 613) states, "The shores of the Cape were, within the remembrance of persons now living, strewed in places with huge bones of whales, these remaining unwasted many years. Fifty years back (Ca. 1780) rib-bones set for posts in fencing was no unusual sight." Even today an occasional whale is beached on the shore of Cape Cod or a carcass washes ashore and causes a major sanitary problem.

MOURT'S
RELATION:
A JOURNAL
OF THE
PILGRIMS OF
PLYMOUTH

A RELATION OR
JOURNAL OF THE
PROCEEDINGS OF
THE PLANTATION
SETTLED AT
PLYMOUTH IN
NEW ENGLAND

winter to fish for whale here. For cod we assayed, but found none; there is good store, no doubt, in their season.[18] Neither got we any fish all the time we lay there, but some few little ones on the shore. We found great mussels,[19] and very fat and full of sea-pearl; but we could not eat them, for they made us all sick that did eat, as well sailors as passengers. They caused to cast and scour; but they were soon well again.

The bay is so round and circling, that before we could come to anchor, we went round all the points of the compass. We could not come near the shore by three quarters of an English mile, because of shallow water;[20] which was a great prejudice to us; for our people, going on shore, were forced to wade a bowshot or two in going a land, which caused many to get colds and coughs; for it was many times freezing cold weather.

This day, before we came to harbor, observing some not well affected to unity and concord, but gave some appearance of faction,[21] it was thought good there should be an association and agreement, that we should combine together in one body,[22] and to submit to such government and governors as we should by common consent agree to make and choose, and set our hands to this that follows, word for word.

In the name of God, Amen. We, whose names are underwritten, the loyal subjects of our dread sovereign lord, King James, by the grace of God, of Great Britain,

18. Young writes (p. 119): "This is a little remarkable; for cod are caught at the Cape as early as November. They probably fished only in the harbor. The best season is in February and March, when they are caught in great plenty between Race Point and Wood End," and Dexter explains (p. 4), "It is not likely that they fished outside of the harbor; nor would they have caught cod, even there, at that time of the year. They probably took only the small 'bar-fish,' as they are now called, which are caught in the east end of the harbor."

19. "Dr. Freeman and Dr. Young supposed that the giant clam, or sea-hen (*mactra solidissima*) is here referred to. But Captain Smith—whose *Description of New England,* published in 1616, must have been in the hands of the *Mayflower,* and their chief authority and guide—speaks of clams (*clampus*) as found, with lobsters, in almost all the sandy bays; so that they would most likely have known that fish by that name. Mussels (*mytilus edulis*) they were familiar with at home; and as these are found in abundance about low-water mark in Long Point, near their anchorage, while the giant clam is only found on the bars at the east end of Provincetown, and along the Truro shore, and is accessible only at the lowest tides, and would seem, therefore, to have been so much more removed from their ready discovery, it is most probably that mussels, of a size to them unfamiliar,—probably the *mytilus modiolus,*—were what they meant. The hearty eating of these, after sixty-four days of salt provender, might produce the described effect upon their systems; indeed, under any circumstances, at certain seasons, such results might follow . . . The mention of 'pearls'—which are plentifully found in mussels, but not in clams—confirms this view." (Dexter, p. 4)

20. Young states, "At the head of the harbor, towards Wood End, and at East Harbor, the flats extend three quarters of a mile from the shore. They also lie along the shore in front of the town, but do not extend so far from the land. At low water it is very shallow, and it is still necessary to wade a considerable distance, to get into a boat. . . ." (pp. 120-121)

21. Bradford writes, "I shall a little return back and begin with a combination made by them before they came ashore, being the first foundation of the government in the place; occasioned partly by the discontented and mutinous speeches that some of the strangers amongst them had let fall from them in the ship, that when they came ashore they would use their own liberty, for none had power to command them, the patent they had being for Virginia and not for New England, which belonged to another government, with which the Virginia Company had nothing to do."

22. Young presents a cogent argument (pp. 120-121), "Here, for the first time in the world's history, the philosophical fiction of a social compact was realized in practice. And yet it seems to me that a great deal more has been discerned in this document than the signers contemplated." He points out that John Robinson, the spiritual leader of the Pilgrims, had indicated in his letter upon their departure that "you are to become a body politic, using amongst yourselves civil government," and Young asserts, "Their purpose in drawing up and signing this compact was simply, as they state, to restrain certain of their number, who had manifested an unruly and factious disposition. This was the whole philosophy of the instrument, whatever may since have been discovered and deduced from it by astute civilians, philosophical historians, and imaginative orators."

MOURT'S
RELATION:
A JOURNAL
OF THE
PILGRIMS OF
PLYMOUTH

A RELATION OR
JOURNAL OF THE
PROCEEDINGS OF
THE PLANTATION
SETTLED AT
PLYMOUTH IN
NEW ENGLAND

France, and Ireland king, defender of the faith, &c., having undertaken, for the glory of God, and advancement of the Christian faith, and[23] honor of our King and country, a voyage to plant the first colony in the northern parts of Virginia, do, by these presents, solemnly and mutually, in the presence of God and one of[24] another, covenant and combine ourselves together into a civil body politic, for our better ordering and preservation, and furtherance of the ends aforesaid; and by virtue hereof to[25] enact, constitute and frame such just and equal laws, ordinances, acts, constitutions,[26] and offices, from time to time, as shall be thought most meet and convenient for the general good of the colony; unto which we promise all due submission and obedience. In witness whereof we have hereunder[27] subscribed our names,[28] at Cape Cod,[29] (the) 11th of November, in the year of[30] the reign of our sovereign lord, King James, of England, France and Ireland[31] (the) eighteenth, and of Scotland the fifty-fourth, *anno Domini* 1620.[32]

The same day,[33] so soon as we could, we set ashore fifteen or sixteen men, well armed, with some to fetch wood, for we had none left, as also to see what the land was, and what inhabitants they could meet with. They found it[34] to be a small neck of land;[35] on this side where we lay, is the bay,[36] and the further side the sea;[37] the ground or earth sand hills, much like the downs[38] in Holland, but much better;[39] the crust of the earth, a spit's depth,[40] excellent black earth;[41] all wooded[42] with oaks, pines, sassafras, juniper, birch, holly, vines, some ash, walnut;[43] the wood for the

---

23. Nathaniel Morton (*New Englands Memoriall,* p. 15) inserts "the" here.

24. Here N. Morton inserts "of."

25. N. Morton uses "do" instead of "to."

26. N. Morton inserts "here" at this point as does Bradford in his manuscript of *Of Plimoth Plantation.*

27. N. Morton substitutes "hereunto."

28. N. Morton lists the names of forty-one signers.

29. The word "the" does not appear in the original printing of the Compact in *Mourt's Relation* in 1622, but both Bradford and N. Morton insert the word.

30. N. Morton omits the words "the year of."

31. Both Bradford and N. Morton insert "the" here. In the original printing of *Mourt's Relation* (1622), the years are given as "18" and "54," while Bradford and Morton write "the 18th" and "the 54th."

32. The date, new style, is November 21, 1620.

33. John Carver after this was confirmed as Governor.

34. Both Young and Freeman identify the land as Long Point, which, according to Freeman, "tradition says has been diminished in its length, breadth, and height."

35. Dexter does not agree with Young and Freeman. He writes (p. 10), "But it seems to me far from improbable that their explorations extended across the end of the Cape, between Race Point and Wood's End, so that by the sea on 'the further side' they meant the Atlantic and not 'Barnstable Bay.'"

36. The word "bay" in this instance refers to the harbor.

37. Cape Cod Bay.

38. Dexter notes (p. 40), "That part of Holland with which the Pilgrims had become familiar, skirting the North Sea, abounds in sand dunes similar to those on the New England coast; it being estimated that they have an extent there of 140,000 acres."

39. Young points out that several European countries plant "sea-reed grass to arrest the sand and form soil on the shore" and that in the 1830's a similar practice was begun on Cape Cod by planting beach grass (psamma arenaria).

40. The depth of a spade.

41. Both Young and Dexter point out that the black earth is the result of thousands of years of vegetable mold as well as clam beds eventually covered by sand. Dexter indicates that the removal of trees has been responsible for the "change from that day of fertility to the present extensive barrenness and desolation of the Cape." Dexter wrote this in 1865.

42. Dexter adds (pp. 10-11) that there were not only the trees indicated, but the Cape also abounded in grapes, greenberries, Virginia creeper, honeysuckle, and poison ivy.

43. There are still example of all of these trees and shrubs on Cape Cod.

most part open and without underwood,[44] fit either to go or ride in. At night our people returned, but found not any person, nor habitation; and laded their boat with juniper,[45] which smelled very sweet and strong, and of which we burnt the most part of the time we lay there.

Monday,[46] the 13th of November.[47] We unshipped our shallop, and drew her on land, to mend and repair her, having been forced to cut her down in bestowing her betwixt the decks, and she was much opened with the people's lying in her;[48] which kept us long there, for it was sixteen or seventeen days before the carpenter had finished her. Our people went on shore to refresh themselves, and our women to wash, as they had great need.[49] But whilst we lay thus still, hoping our shallop would be ready in five or six days at the furthest, (but our carpenter made slow work of it, so that) some of our people, impatient of delay, desired for our better furtherance to travel by land unto the country, (which was not without appearance of danger, not having the shallop with them, nor means to carry provision but on their backs) to see whether it might to fit for us to seat in or no; and the rather, because, as we sailed into the harbor, there seemed to be a river opening itself into the main land.[50] The willingness of the persons was liked, but the thing itself, in regard to the danger, was rather permitted than approved; and so with cautions, directions, and instructions, sixteen men were set out, with every man his musket, sword, and corselet,[51] under the conduct of Captain Miles Standish,[52] unto whom was adjoined, for counsel and advice, William Bradford,[53]

44. Captain John Smith in 1614 indicated that Cape Cod was "a headland of high hills of sand, overgrown with shrubby pines, hurts and such trash."

45. In 1602, Bartholomew Gosnold collected "cypress, birch, witchhazel, and beech for firewood on this end of the Cape."

46. They probably spent Sunday on board the *Mayflower*.

47. New style, November 23, 1620.

48. Bradford wrote, "They having brought a large shallop with them out of England, stowed in quarters in the ship, they now got her out and set their carpenters to work to trim her up; but being much bruised and shattered in the ship with foul weather, they saw she would be long in mending."

49. For more than three centuries New England children have been taught that this was the first "Blue Monday" and that the custom of doing the laundry on Mondays began with the Pilgrim women.

50. The Pamet River.

51. Young notes, "Their guns were Matchlocks, as appears from their 'having five or six inches of match burning,' Nov. 16, and from their 'lighting all their matches,' Nov. 30." (p. 125). Dexter defines the corselet as "a piece of defensive armor covering the breast from the neck to the girdle; in distinction from the cuirass, which added a back piece buckled on each side to the corselet."

52. Myles Standish, the military leader of Plymouth Colony, was born in Lancashire about 1584. He served as soldier for the Dutch in the war with Spain, and, during the twelve-year truce, he met the Pilgrims in Leyden, although he did not join their church. He came to the New World with his wife Rose, who died in the first sickness. In 1623 he married Barbara _____, who probably came over on the *Anne*. His whole life in Plymouth was devoted to public service. In 1625 and 1628 he was sent to England on public business, and in 1631 he moved to Duxbury. He was captain and military leader after 1621, an assistant to the governor for nineteen years, treasurer of the colony for six years, and in 1649 he was made Commander-in-Chief for the colony. He died at Duxbury, on October 3/13, 1656.

53. William Bradford was born in Austerfield, Yorkshire, on March 29, 1590 (n.s.). A member of the original congregation in Scrooby, he went to Amsterdam and later to Leyden with the group. On December 10, 1613, (n.s.) he married Dorothy May, who was drowned in Cape Cod December 7/17, 1620. When Governor Carver died in the early spring of 1620, Bradford was chosen to succeed him, and from this time to his death in 1657 he was elected governor each year except 1633, 1634, 1636, 1638, 1644. In these latter years he was elected Assistant. He married on August 14/24, 1623 Alice Carpenter Southworth, who had come over on the *Anne*. He wrote *Of Plimoth Plantation*, which was first printed in 1856, three dialogues, a number of letters, and a calendar of the early days in Plymouth. This last item has been lost for more than 200 years. He died in Plymouth May 9/19, 1657, at the age of 67.

MOURT'S
RELATION:
A JOURNAL
OF THE
PILGRIMS OF
PLYMOUTH

A RELATION OR
JOURNAL OF THE
PROCEEDINGS OF
THE PLANTATION
SETTLED AT
PLYMOUTH IN
NEW ENGLAND

Stephen Hopkins,[54] and Edward Tilley.[55]

Wednesday, the 15th of November. They were set ashore;[56] and when they had ordered themselves in the order of a single file and marched about the space of a mile by the sea,[57] they espied five or six people with a dog coming towards them, who were savages; who, when they saw them, ran into the wood,[58] and whistled the dog after them, &c. First they supposed them to be Master Jones, the master,[59] and some of his men, for they were ashore and knew of their coming; but after they knew them to be Indians, they marched after them into the woods,[60] lest other of the Indians should lie in ambush. But when the Indians saw our men following them, they ran away with might and main; and our men turned out of the wood after them, for it was they intended to go,[61] but they could not come near them. They followed them that night about ten miles[62] by the trace of their footings, and saw how they had come the same way they went,[63] and at a turning perceived how they ran up a hill,[64] to see whether they followed them. At length night came upon them, and they were constrained to take up their lodging.[65] So they set forth three sentinels; and the rest, some kindled a fire, and others fetched wood, and there held our rendezvous that night.[66]

In the morning,[67] so soon as we could see the trace, we proceeded on our journey and had the track until we had compassed the head of a long creek;[68] and there they

---

54. Stephen Hopkins was'a Londoner, who had undoubtedly been in America about 1609-1610 and came to the New World with the Pilgrims to protect the investors' interests. He took part in the early explorations of Cape Cod and Plymouth and was chosen an assistant annually from 1633 to 1636 and as a member of the Council of War for Plymouth Colony from 1642 to 1644. He died in Plymouth early in the summer of 1644.

55. Edward Tilley came to Plymouth with his wife and two children who were their cousins, Henry Sampson and Cooper. He went on the third expedition which left the *Mayflower* in the shallop which had the first encounter with the Indians and explored Plymouth harbor. He, his wife and the children all died that first winter.

56. November 25, 1620. Dexter believes (p. 15) that they were set ashore "somewhere near the present site of the village of Provincetown, most likely on the western end of the beach where the women washed their clothes, near Payne's Hill."

57. Near the crest of the present-day High Hill.

58. The "wood" referred to was probably around Duck Pond, which was in those days densely wooded.

59. The Christian name of "Mr. Jones, the master" does not appear in any work by the original Pilgrims. Later research indicates that his name was "Christopher." Nathanial Morton in his *New Englands Memoriall* accuses Jones of being bribed by the Dutch to keep the Pilgrims out of the Hudson River area where they originally intended to settle.

60. Dexter points out (p. 15) that the Indians entered the woods, "and then ran out of them around the north end of Great Pond over toward Negro Head, and so to the east towards Truro."

61. According to Dexter (p. 16), if the exploring party had surveyed the western half of Provincetown as he suggests, then, "it would be natural that they should now intend to survey the eastern; which would lead them over between Dutch and Great ponds to the ocean side, as they now went, after the Indians."

62. Both Dexter (p. 16) and Young (pp. 127-128) agree that the heavy equipment that the men carried made the distance seem longer. Dexter estimates that "This party, if they followed the Indians north between the ponds, and then east to the neighborhood of Stout's Creek—making allowance for all their probably windings,—must have marched not far from seven miles before they encamped for the night."

63. The Indian tracks coming and going obviously indicate that the Indians had seen the ships, decided to investigate, and then returned home when they were sighted.

64. Dexter believes (p. 16) that if his theory that the party followed this route is correct, the hill was Negro Head, eighty-eight feet high. Young points out that it might have been Snow's Hill, Mt. Gillboa, or Mt. Ararat.

65. Probably near Stout's Creek, formerly a small branch of East Harbor Creek in Truro. The area, formerly a salt marsh, is now covered over by sand.

66. The night of Wednesday, November 15/25, 1620.

67. Thursday, November 16/26, 1620.

68. East Harbor Creek, about three and one-half miles distant.

MOURT'S
RELATION:
A JOURNAL
OF THE
PILGRIMS OF
PLYMOUTH

A RELATION OR
JOURNAL OF THE
PROCEEDINGS OF
THE PLANTATION
SETTLED AT
PLYMOUTH IN
NEW ENGLAND

took into another wood,[69] and we after them, supposing to find some of their dwellings. But we marched through boughs and bushes, and under hills and valleys, which tore our very armor in pieces,[70] and yet could meet with none of them, nor their houses, nor find any fresh water, which we greatly desired and stood in need of; for we brought neither beer nor water with us, and our victuals was only biscuit and Holland cheese, and a little bottle of aquavitae,[71] so as we were sore athirst. About ten o'clock we came into a deep valley,[72] full of brush, woodgaile,[73] and long grass,[74] through which we found little paths or tracks and there we saw a deer[75] and found springs of fresh water,[76] of which we were heartily glad, and sat us down and drunk our first New England water, with as much delight as ever we drunk drink in all our lives.[77]

When we had refreshed ourselves, we directed our course full south,[78] that we might come to the shore, which within a short while after we did, and there made a fire, that they in the ship might see where we were, as we had direction;[79] and so marched on towards this supposed river. And as we went, in another valley we found a fine clear pond of fresh water, being about a musket shot broad, and twice as long.[80] There grew also many small vines, and fowl and deer haunted there. There grew much sassafras.[81] From thence we went on, and found much plain ground,[82] about fifty acres, fit for the plough, and some signs where the Indians had formerly planted their corn.[83] After this, some thought it best, for nearness of the river, to go

---

69. Dexter notes (p. 17) that, "Clearing the end of East Harbor Creek, they turned toward the south, which would bring them toward the woods, which seem to have covered the ridges and central portion—back from the ocean on the n.e. and the bay on the s.w."

70. Dr. Freeman wrote in 1801, "Excepting the trees and bushes, which have disappeared, this is an exact description of that part of Truro called East Harbor."

71. A liqueur made of "brewed beer, strongly hopp'd, well fermented."

72. The present-day village of East Harbor in Truro.

73. Probably sweet-gale or Dutch mrytle (*myrica gale*), according to Young, but Dexter thinks the reference is to bayberry (*myrica cerifera*) which abounds on the Cape.

74. A general name for various types of bushes, wild-roses, whortleberry, blueberry, beach-plum and other shrubs along the coast.

75. Despite the extensive settlement of the Cape, deer are still sighted there.

76. This water no longer exists. In 1801 Freeman refered to it as Dyer's Swamp but the swamp has been completely obliterated.

77. Most colonial explorers commented favorably upon the excellence of the water in New England. Brereton in 1602 comments on the "many springs of excellent sweet water" on the Elizabeth Islands, and Captain John Smith wrote of "the waters most pure, proceeding from the entrails of rocky mountains."

78. The course from Dyer's swamp to the Pond is south according to Freeman.

79. Bradford, who undoubtedly wrote this account, states in his *Of Plimoth Plantation*, "Afterwards they directed their course to come to the other shore, for they knew it was a neck of land they were to cross over, and so at length got to the seaside." Dexter adds (p. 18), "A s.w. course would bring them to the shore of the bay within the distance of a mile from Dyer's Swamp; while their fire built there on the shore could not have been distant much more than four miles across the bay, very nearly due e. from the anchorage of the *Mayflower.*"

80. This pond, about a mile south of the village of East Harbor, gave the name Pond Village to this section of Truro.

81. The root and bark of the sassafras plant in the sixteenth and seventeenth centuries were thought to contain great medicinal virtues. Gosnold in 1602 partly loaded his vessel with sassafras from Cuttyhunk, for in that year the root sold in England for three shillings a pound.

82. Freeman indicates that the "land on the south side of the Pond is an elevated plain." Dexter (p. 19) points out that "proceeding southward toward Pamet River, of which they were in search, they would next come to a section of elevated tableland, now traceable between Pond Village and Great Hollow."

83. This is the first mention of the basic crop of North American Indians in their work. Indian corn (*zea mays*) was the salvation of the Pilgrims in the early years.

MOURT'S
RELATION:
A JOURNAL
OF THE
PILGRIMS OF
PLYMOUTH

A RELATION OR
JOURNAL OF THE
PROCEEDINGS OF
THE PLANTATION
SETTLED AT
PLYMOUTH IN
NEW ENGLAND

down and travel on the sea sands, by which means some of our men were tired, and lagged behind. So we stayed and gathered them up, and struck into the land again;[84] where we found a little path to certain heaps of sand, one whereof was covered with old mats, and had a wooden thing, like a mortar, whelmed on the top of it, and an earthen pot laid in a little hole at the end thereof. We, musing that it might be, digged and found a bow, and, as we thought, arrows, but they were rotten. We supposed there were many other things; but because we deemed them graves,[85] we put in the bow again, and made it up as it was, and left the rest untouched, because we thought it would be odious unto them to ransack their sepulchres.

We went on further and found new stubble, of which they had gotten corn this year, and many walnut trees[86] full of nuts, and great store of strawberries,[87] and some vines.[88] Passing thus a field or two, which were not great, we came to another,[89] which had also been new gotten,[90] and there we found where a house had been, and four or five old planks laid together.[91] Also we found a great kettle, which had been some ship's kettle, and brought out of Europe. There was also a heap of sand[92] made like the former,—but it was newly done, we might see how they had

84. Freeman indicates that this was "probably at the Great Hollow." This place is indicated by Young (p. 131) as "a mile south of the Pond village, the bank on the bay is intersected by another valley called the Great Hollow."

85. Dexter quotes (p. 20) Schoolcraft's *History of the Indian Tribes of the United States* (II, 69) to indicate that Indians "choose dry and elevated places for burial, which are completely out of the reach of floods or standing water" and Roger Williams, who wrote in his *Key into the Language of America,* "Upon the Grave is spread the Mat that the party died on, the dish he ate in, &c."

86. These trees differed from the English walnut trees, as several early observers of New England noted. Dexter believes (p. 20) these trees were the Mockernut hickory variety (*carya tomentosa*) which still grows in eastern and southern Massachusetts. The fruit ripen in October so there would still be nuts on the trees.

87. The wild strawberry (*fragaria Virginiana*) was the subject of many rhapsodic paragraphs by New England observers. William Wood in his *New England's Prospect* (1634) writes, "There is strawberries in abundance, very large ones, some being two inches about; one may gather half a bushel in a forenoon." Roger Williams in his *Key . . .* writes, "This berry is the wonder of all the fruits, growing naturally in those parts. In some places where the natives have planted, I have many times seen as many as would fill a good ship within a few miles' compass." As late as 1855, Henry David Thoreau in his *Cape Cod* wrote, "Strawberries grew there abundantly in the little hollows on the edge of the desert, standing amid the beach-grass in the sand."

88. Observers also noted the abundance of grapes. Thomas Morton in his *New English Canaan* (Ch. 2) wrote, "Of this kind of trees, there are that bear grapes of three colors, that is to say white, black and red. The country is so apt for vines that, but for the fire at the spring of the year, the vines would so overspread the land that one should not be able to pass for them; the fruit is as big as some as a musket bullet, and is excellent in taste." In his *New England's Prospect* (Ch. 5), William Wood writes, "The vines afford great store of grapes, which are very big both for grape and cluster, sweet and good. These be of two sorts, red and white. There is likewise a smaller kind of grape, which groweth in the islands, which is sooner ripe, and more delectable."

89. Young writes (p. 133), "From the Great Hollow the sixteen adventurers travelled south to the hill which terminates in Hopkins's Cliff (or Uncle Sam's hill, as it is now vulgarly called.) This they called Cornhill. The Indians formerly dwelt in great number on this hill; and the shells deposited by them on it, are still ploughed up in abundance. Hopkins's creek, or Pamet's little river, as it is now called."

90. That is, another field where the stubble showed that the Indians had recently "gotten corn."

91. Bradford in his *Of Plimoth Plantation* writes that about 1617 "a French ship was cast away at Cape Cod, but the men got ashore, and saved their lives, and much of their victuals and other goods." This was probably the remains of their hut.

92. Young (p. 133) quotes Thomas Morton and William Wood. Morton wrote in *New English Canaan* (Ch. 13), "Their barns are holes made in the earth, that will hold a hogshead of corn apiece. In these, when their corn is out of the husk, and well dried, they lay their store in great baskets, with mats under, about the sides, and on the top; and putting it into the place made for it, they cover it with earth, and in this manner it is preserved from destruction or putrefaction, to be used in case of necessity, and not else." William Wood in *New England's Prospect* (Ch. 20) wrote, "Their corn being ripe, they gather it, and dry it in the sun, convey it to their barns, which be great holes digged in the ground, in form of a brass pot, ceiled with rinds of trees, wherein they put their corn."

MOURT'S
RELATION:
A JOURNAL
OF THE
PILGRIMS OF
PLYMOUTH

A RELATION OR
JOURNAL OF THE
PROCEEDINGS OF
THE PLANTATION
SETTLED AT
PLYMOUTH IN
NEW ENGLAND

paddled it with their hands,—which we digged up, and in it we found a little old basket, full of fair Indian corn; and digged further, and found a fine great new basket, full of very fair corn of this year, with some six and thirty goodly ears of corn, some yellow, and some red, and others mixed with blue,[93] which was a very goodly sight. The basket[94] was round, and narrow at the top. It held about three or four bushels, which was as much as two of us could lift up from the ground, and was very handsomely and cunningly made.[95] But whilst we were busy about these things, we set our men sentinel in a round ring, all but two or three which digged up the corn. We were in suspense what to do with it and the kettle; and at length, after much consultation, we concluded to take the kettle, and as much of the corn as we could carry away with us; and when our shallop came, if we could find any of the people and come to parley with them, we would give them the kettle again, and satisfy them for their corn.[96] So we took all the ears, and put a good deal of the loose corn in the kettle, for two men to bring away on a staff. Besides, they that could put any into their pockets, filled the same. The rest we buried again; for we were so laden with armor that we could carry no more.

Not far from this place we found the remainder of an old fort or palisado, which, as we conceived, had been made by some Christian.[97] This was also hard by that place which we thought had been a river; unto which we went, and found it so to be, dividing itself into two arms by a high bank,[98] standing right by the cut or mouth, which came from the sea.[99] That which was next unto us was the less.[100] The other arm[101] was more than twice as big, and not unlike to be a harbor for ships; but whether it be a fresh river, or only an indraught of the sea, we had not time to discover; for we had commandment to be out but two days. Here also we saw two canoes;[102] the one on the one side, the other on the other side.[103] We could not believe it was a canoe, till we came near it. So we returned, leaving the further discovery hereof to our shallop, and came that night back again to the fresh water pond;[104] and there we made our rendezvous that night, making a great fire, and a

---

93. Mixed-color corn—yellow, red, and blue is not uncommon even today in southeastern Massachusetts.

94. See description of baskets in note 92. (p. 18)

95. Other observers noted the Indian baskets. Wood wrote in *New England's Prospect* (Ch. 30), "In summer they gather flags, of which they make mats for houses, and hemp and ruskes, with dyeing stuff of which they make curious baskets, with intermixed colors, and portraitures of antique imagery. These baskets be all sizes from a quart to a quarter, in which they carry their luggage." Roger Williams in his *Key* . . . wrote, "Instead of shelves, they have several baskets, wherein they put all their household stuff. They have some great bags or sacks, made of hemp, which will hold five or six bushels."

96. This was done within six months.

97. Both Dexter and Young believe that the people who built the hut and left the kettle constructed this palisado.

98. Dexter (p. 22) identifies this as Old Tom's Hill in Indian Neck. Young says that the hill is named for an Indian chief who formerly lived here. It is at the entrance of the Pamet River.

99. Bradford says, "This was near the place of that supposed river they came to seek; unto which they went and found it to open itself into two arms with a high cliff of sand, in the entrance but more like to be creeks of salt water than any fresh, for aught they saw."

100. Dexter (p. 23) identifies the "*less*" arm as "Hopkins's Creek, North Branch, or Pamet Little River."

101. The other arm "was Pamet River, or Pamet Creek, or Pamet harbor, which almost cuts off the cape here, terminating only within a few rods of the eastern shore." (Dexter, p. 23)

102. The natives at this time used both bark canoes and dugouts.

103. What is meant is not clear, although Young interprets this to mean on either side of Old Tom's Hill.

104. The pond at Pond Village. See note 80. (p. 17)

MOURT'S
RELATION:
A JOURNAL
OF THE
PILGRIMS OF
PLYMOUTH

A RELATION OR
JOURNAL OF THE
PROCEEDINGS OF
THE PLANTATION
SETTLED AT
PLYMOUTH IN
NEW ENGLAND

barricade[105] to windward of us, and kept good watch with three sentinels all night, every one standing when his turn came, while five or six inches of match[106] was burning. It proved a very rainy night.

In the morning,[107] we took our kettle and sunk it in the pond, and trimmed our muskets, for few of them would go off because of the wet; and so coasted the wood[108] again to come home, in which we were shrewdly puzzled, and lost our way. As we wandered we came to a tree, where a young spirit[109] was bowed down over a bow, and some acorns strewed underneath. Stephen Hopkins said, it had been to catch some deer. So as we were looking at it, William Bradford being in the rear, when he came looked also upon it, and as he went about, it gave a sudden jerk up, and he was immediately caught by the leg.[110] It was a very pretty device, made with a rope of their own making and having a noose as artificially made as any roper[111] in England can make, and as like ours as can be; which we brought away with us. In the end we got out of the wood, and were fallen about a mile too high above the creek;[112] where we saw three bucks,[113] but we had rather have had one of them.[114] We also did spring three couple of partridges;[115] and as we came along by the creek, we saw great flocks of wild geese and ducks,[116] but they were very fearful of us. So we marched some while in the woods, some while on the sands, and other while in the water up to the knees;[117] till at length we came near the ship;[118] and then we shot off our pieces, and the long boat came to fetch us. Master Jones and Master Carver being on the shore, with many of our people, came to meet us. And thus we came both weary and welcome home;[119] and delivered in our corn into the store to be kept for seed, for we

---

105. Bradford describes the event as follows: "So they made them a barricado (as usually they did every night) with logs, stakes, and thick pine boughs, the height of a man, leaving it open to leeward, partly to shelter them from the cold and wind (making their fire in the middle and lying round about it), and partly to defend them from any assaults of the savages, if they should surround them."

106. This is further proof that most of their weapons were matchlocks, which would have been worthless in a sudden attack unless the match were kept ignited.

107. Friday, November 17/27, 1620.

108. Freeman writes, "The wood was terminated by the Pond, by the side of which they travelled, and then through a valley, which is continued from it, east, toward the ocean."

109. A sprout, a young sapling.

110. W. Wood writes (Ch. 15) that "their deer traps are springs made of young trees and smooth wrought cords; so strong as it will toss a horse if he be caught in it." Thomas Morton (Ch. 5) writes that, "The savages take the deer in traps made of their natural hemp, which they place in the earth, where they fell a tree for browse; and when he rounds the tree for the browse, if he tread on the trap, he is horsed up by the leg, by means of a pole that starts up and catcheth him."

111. Ropemaker.

112. Dexter writes (p. 25), "This would indicate that they came out upon the eastern shore, scarcely three quarters of a mile n.w. of the present site (1865) of the Highland Light."

113. See note 75. (p. 17)

114. Dexter points this out as an example of grim Pilgrim humor.

115. The *perdix Virginiana,* the partridge or quail, as it is called in New England, is still found in southeastern Massachusetts.

116. Young (p. 137) identifies these as the Canada goose (*anser Canadiensis*) and the dusky duck (*anas obscura*).

117. Dexter (pp. 25-26) takes issue with Young's theory that the party went down the west side of East Harbor Creek and forded its mouth. He offers several good points to defend his contention and concludes "that they went back by essentially the same way that they had come."

118. Young seems to believe that the *Mayflower* was about two miles from Provincetown, but Dr. Dexter (pp. 26-27) is convinced that the ship was less than a mile from shore. From the internal evidence in this work, this editor is inclined to agree with Dexter.

119. They had been away three days.

MOURT'S
RELATION:
A JOURNAL
OF THE
PILGRIMS OF
PLYMOUTH

A RELATION OR
JOURNAL OF THE
PROCEEDINGS OF
THE PLANTATION
SETTLED AT
PLYMOUTH IN
NEW ENGLAND

knew not how to come by any, and therefore were very glad, purposing, so soon as we could meet with any of the inhabitants of that place, to make them large satisfaction. This was our first discovery, whilst our shallop was in repairing.

Our people did make things as fitting as they could, and time would, in seeking out wood, and helving of tools, and sawing of timber, to build a new shallop. But the discommodiousness of the harbor did much hinder us; for we could neither go to nor come from the shore but at high water, which was much to our hindrance and hurt; for oftentimes they waded to the middle of the thigh, and oft to the knees, to go and come from land.[120] Some did it necessarily, and some for their own pleasure; but it brought to the most, if not to all, coughs and colds, (the weather proving suddenly cold and stormy,) which afterwards turned to the scurvy, whereof many died.

When our shallop was fit, (indeed before she was fully fitted, for there was two days' work after bestowed on her,) there was appointed some four and twenty men of our own, and armed, then to go and make a more full discovery of the rivers before mentioned.[121] Master Jones was desirous to go with us, and we took such of his sailors as he thought useful for us; as we were in all about thirty-four men.[122] We made Master Jones our leader; for we thought it best herein to gratify his kindness and forwardness.[123] When we set forth,[124] it proved rough weather and cross winds; so as we were constrained, some in the shallop, and others in the long boat, to row to the nearest shore the wind would suffer them to go unto, and then to wade out above the knees.[125] The wind was so strong as the shallop could not keep the water, but was forced to harbor there that night. But we marched six or seven miles further, and appointed the shallop to come to us as soon as they could. It blowed and did snow all that day and night, and froze withal. Some of our people that are dead took the original of their death here.[126]

The next day,[127] about eleven o'clock, our shallop came to us, and we shipped ourselves; and the wind being good, we sailed to the river we formerly discovered,[128] which we named *Cold Harbor;* to which when we came, we found it not navigable for ships; yet we thought it might be a good harbor for boats, for it flows there twelve foot at high water.[129] We landed our men between the two creeks,[130] and marched some four or five miles[131] by the greater of them,[132] and the shallop followed us. At

---

120. See note 20. (p. 13)

121. Pamet River and its three branches.

122. Including ten of the *Mayflower's* crew.

123. Both Young and Dexter indicate that this shows that the Pilgrims had no suspicion that Jones had betrayed them. See note 59. (p. 16)

124. This is now ten days after their return. Monday, November 27/December 7, 1620. They probably spent Sunday on the *Mayflower.*

125. According to Dexter, this is probably Beach Point. (p. 28)

126. Dexter believes (p. 28) that "They probably did not get farther from Beach Point than Great Hollow, where they might conveniently take the shallop next day; which would be about five miles."

127. Tuesday, November 28/December 8, 1620.

128. Pamet River.

129. Freeman writes, "The mouth of Pamet river is twelve feet at high water. Thence the water gradually decreases to five feet, which is the depth at the lower bridge. This is to be understood of the lowest tides, during the summer."

130. Old Tom's Hill, or Indian Neck.

131. Freeman writes, "From Old Tom's hill to the head of Pamet river the distance is about three miles and a half, as the hills run, or three miles in a straight line. The tradition is that Pamet river was formerly deeper than it is at present, and therefore the shallop might easily follow them."

132. Dexter indicates that this estimate is an exaggeration and that "we must make some allowance for the influence of circumstances upon miles." (p. 29)

MOURT'S
RELATION:
A JOURNAL
OF THE
PILGRIMS OF
PLYMOUTH

A RELATION OR
JOURNAL OF THE
PROCEEDINGS OF
THE PLANTATION
SETTLED AT
PLYMOUTH IN
NEW ENGLAND

length night grew on, and our men were tired with marching up and down the steep hills and deep valleys,[133] which lay half a foot thick with snow. Master Jones, wearied with marching, was desirous we should take up our lodging, though some of us would have marched further. So we made there our rendezvous for that night under a few pine trees; and as it fell out, we got three fat geese,[134] and six ducks[135] to our supper, which we eat with soldiers' stomachs, for we had eaten little all that day. Our resolution was, next morning to go up to the head of this river, for we supposed it would prove fresh water.[136]

But in the morning[137] our resolution held not, because many liked not the hilliness of the soil and badness of the harbor. So we turned towards the other creek,[138] that we might go over and look for the rest of the corn that we left behind when we were here before. When we came to the creek, we saw the canoe[139] lie on the dry ground, and a flock of geese in the river, at which one made a shot and killed a couple of them; and we launched the canoe and fetched them, and when we had done, she carried us over by seven or eight at once. This done, we marched to the place where we had the corn formerly, which place we called *Cornhill;* and digged and found the rest, of which we were very glad. We also digged in a place a little further off, and found a bottle of oil.[140] We went to another place, which we had seen before, and digged and found more corn, *viz.* two or three baskets full of Indian wheat,[141] and a bag of beans, with a good many of fair wheat ears.[142] Whilst some of us were digging up this, some others found another heap of corn, which they digged up also; so as we had in all about ten bushels, which will serve us sufficiently for seed. And sure it was God's good Providence that we found this corn, for else we know not how we should have done; for we knew not how we should find or meet with any of the Indians, except it be to do us a mischief. Also, we had never in all likelihood seen a grain of it, if we had not made our first journey;[143] for the ground was now covered

---

133. Freeman points out that "This is an exact description of the land of Pamet river," and Young adds, "Truro is composed of hills and narrow circular valleys. There are also some long valleys, running at right angles with the shore. The tops of some of the hills spread out into a plain." (p. 139)

134. Several authors have commented on the geese and ducks of the area. Josselyn wrote, "There are three kinds of goose, the gray goose, the white goose, and the brant." Thomas Morton wrote in *New English Canaan* (Ch. 4), "There are geese of three sorts, viz, brant geese, which are pied, and white geese, which are bigger, and gray geese which are as big and bigger than the tame geese of England, with black legs, black bills, heads and necks black; the flesh far more excellent than the geese of England, wild or tame. There is of them great abundance; I have had often a thousand before the mouth of my gun." Wood (Ch. 3) verifies Morton's statement and adds that "most of these geese remain with us from Michelmas to April. They feed on the sea, upon the grass in bays at low water, and gravel, and in the woods of acorns, having, as other fowl do, their pass and repass to the northward and southward."

135. Thomas Morton writes (Ch. 4), "Ducks there are of three kinds, pied ducks, gray ducks, and black ducks, in great abundance; they are bigger bodied than the tame ducks of England." William Wood writes (Ch. 8), "The ducks of the country be very large ones, and in great abundance. So there is of teal likewise. If I should tell you how some have killed a hundred geese in a week, fifty ducks at a shot, forty teal at another, it may be counted almost impossible, though nothing more certain."

136. Dexter writes, "They must have been then within a mile of the Atlantic side. The present isthmus between the head of Pamet River and the beach on the eastern side of the Cape can scarcely be more than forty rods in width."

137. Wednesday, November 29/December 9, 1620.

138. Toward the north branch and Cornhill.

139. See note 102. (p. 19)

140. Probably another relic of the shipwrecked sailors. See note 91. (p. 18)

141. Maize or Indian corn.

142. Ears of corn.

143. The reference is to the first day, November when they found the corn.

MOURT'S
RELATION:
A JOURNAL
OF THE
PILGRIMS OF
PLYMOUTH

A RELATION OR
JOURNAL OF THE
PROCEEDINGS OF
THE PLANTATION
SETTLED AT
PLYMOUTH IN
NEW ENGLAND

with snow, and so hard frozen that we were fain with out cutlasses[144] and short swords to hew and carve the ground a foot deep, and then wrest it up with levers, for we had forgot to bring other tools. Whilst we were in this employment, foul weather being towards,[145] Master Jones was earnest to go aboard; but sundry of us desired to make further discovery, and to find out the Indians' habitations. So we sent home with him our weakest people, and some that were sick,[146] and all the corn; and eighteen of us stayed still and lodged there[147] that night, and desired that the shallop might return to us next day, and bring us some mattocks and spades with them.

The next morning,[148] we followed certain beaten paths and tracks of the Indians into the woods, supposing they would have led us into some town or houses. After we had gone a while, we light upon a very broad beaten path, well nigh two foot broad. Then we lighted all our matches, and prepared ourselves, concluding that we were near their dwellings. But, in the end, we found it to be only a path[149] made to drive deer in, when the Indians hunt, as we supposed.

When we had marched five or six miles into the woods,[150] and could find no signs of any people, we returned again another way; and as we came into the plain ground,[151] we found a place like a grave, but it was much bigger and longer than any we had yet seen. It was also covered with boards, so as we mused what it should be, and resolved to dig it up; where we found first a mat, and under that a fair bow, and then[152] another mat, and under that a board about three quarters[153] long, finely carved and painted; with three tines or broaches[154] on the top, like a crown. Also between the mats we found bowls, trays, dishes, and such like trinkets. At length we came to a fair new mat, and under that two bundles, the one bigger, the other less. We opened the greater, and found in it a great quantity of fine and perfect red powder, and in it the bones and skull of a man. The skull had fine yellow hair still on it, and some of the flesh unconsumed. There was bound up with it a knife, a packneedle,[155] and two or three old iron things. It was bound up in a sailor's canvass cassock[156] and a pair of cloth breeches.[157] The red powder was a kind of embalmment, and yielded a strong, but no offensive smell; it was as fine as any flour. We opened the less bundle likewise, and found of the same powder in it, and the bones and head of a little child. About the legs and other parts of it was bound strings and bracelets of fine white beads.[158] There was also by it a little bow, about three quarters long,

---

144. The author wrote Curtlaxes.

145. Towards, adv. = near at hand, advancing.

146. Sixteen men returned.

147. Near Cornhill.

148. Thursday, November 30/December 10, 1620.

149. The Indians had made a gradually narrowing path between two rows of hedges to trap deer. As the deer come to the narrow gut the Indians shot them.

150. Dexter believes (p. 32) that the direction of their march "was over toward the Atlantic side, somewhere between Small's Hill and Highland Light."

151. The cleared land south of the Pond where they had found graves in their first expedition.

152. In the original edition (1622) p. 11, the word *there* appears, an obvious error.

153. Three quarters of a yard.

154. *Tines* are prongs of a fork. A broach is a spit used for roasting meat.

155. "A large coarse needle for sewing pack-cloth with pack-thread in doing up a package of goods." (Dexter, p. 33)

156. A cassock is a coarse frock or blouse.

157. Obviously a European garment and certainly not one worn by an Indian.

158. Wampum.

MOURT'S
RELATION:
A JOURNAL
OF THE
PILGRIMS OF
PLYMOUTH

A RELATION OR
JOURNAL OF THE
PROCEEDINGS OF
THE PLANTATION
SETTLED AT
PLYMOUTH IN
NEW ENGLAND

and some other odd knacks.[159] We brought sundry of the pretties things away with us, and covered the corpse up again. After this we digged in sundry like places, but found no more corn, nor any thing else but graves.

There was variety of opinions amongst us about the embalmed person. Some thought it was an Indian lord and king. Others said, the Indians have all black hair, and never any was seen with brown or yellow hair. Some thought it was a Christian of some special note, which had died amongst them, and they thus buried him to honor him. Others thought they had killed him, and did it in triumph over him.[160]

Whilst we were thus ranging and searching, two of the sailors which were newly come on the shore[161] by chance espied two houses, which had been lately dwelt in, but the people were gone. They having their pieces, and hearing nobody, entered the houses, and took out some things, and durst not stay, but came again and told us. So some seven or eight of us went with them, and found how we had gone within a flight shot of them before. The houses[162] were made with long young sapling trees bended, and both ends stuck into the ground.[163] They were made round, like unto an arbor, and covered down to the ground with thick and well wrought mats; and the door was not over a yard high, made of a mat to open.[164] The chimney was a wide open hole in the top; for which they had a mat to cover it close when they pleased. One might stand and go upright in them. In the midst of them were four little trunches[165] knocked into the ground, and small sticks laid over, on which they hung their pots, and what they had to seethe. Round about the fire they lay on mats, which are their beds. The houses were double matted; for as they were matted without, so were they within, with newer and fairer mats.[166] In the houses we found wooden bowls, trays, and dishes, earthen pots, hand-baskets made of crab-shells wrought together;[167] also an English pail or bucket;[168] it wanted a bail,[169] but it had

---

159. There is plenty of known evidence about Indian burial customs. Wood (Ch. 19) states, "It is their custom to bury with their deceased friends their bows and arrows, and good store of their wampompeag." T. Morton says (Ch. 17) that "in the grave of the more noble they put a plank in the bottom for the corpse to be laid upon, and on each side a plank, and a plank upon the top, in the form of a chest, before they cover the place with earth." Roger Williams (Ch. 32) writes that "After the dead is laid in the grave, sometimes, in some parts, some goods are cast in them; and upon the grave is spread the mat that the party died on, and the dish he ate in."

160. Dexter (p. 34) believes that "it is made probable" that this was the grave of one of the French sailors shipwrecked several years before. Some questions remain unanswered: What was the embalming powder? Why was a child buried there? If the French sailors were treated, as Bradford stated, "worse than slaves" by the Indians, why was this one given special attention and honor? Finally, Dexter suggests "it may have been a North-men relic."

161. The shallop had taken the sixteen ill men to the *Mayflower* and now returned for the remaining eighteen.

162. There are many descriptions of Indian wigwams. This is an early one.

163. Higginson in *New England's Plantation* writes, "Their houses are very little and homely, being made with small poles pricked into the ground, and so bended and fastened at the tops, and on the sides they are matted with boughs, and covered on the roof with sedge and old mats.

164. Roger Williams' description, "Their door is a hanging mat, which being left up, falls down of itself."

165. A trunch is a stake or a small post.

166. R. Williams writes, "They line them with embroidered mats which the roomers make, and call them *Mannotaubana,* or *Hangings,* which amongst them make as fair a show as hangings with us."

167. The Indians used maple for bowls, clay for pots, wooden eating utensils, and made baskets of rushes, maize husks, wild hemp, and tree bark.

168. Young reasons (p. 144) that the pail "probably belonged to the persons who built the hut and owned the kettle" found earlier.

169. A handle.

two iron ears. There was also baskets of sundry sorts, bigger and some lesser, finer and some coarser. Some were curiously wrought with black and white in pretty works, and sundry other of their household stuff.[170] We found also two or three deer's heads, one whereof had been newly killed, for it was still fresh. There was also a company of deer's feet stuck up in the houses, harts' horns,[171] and eagles' claws,[172] and sundry such like things there was; also two or three baskets full of parched acorns,[173] pieces of fish, and a piece of a broiled herring. We found also a little silk grass,[174] and a little tobacco seed,[175] with some other seeds which we knew not. Without was sundry bundles of flags, and sedge, bulrushes, and other stuff to make mats.[176] There was thrust into a hollow tree two or three pieces of venison; but we thought it fitter for the dogs than for us. Some of the best things we took away with us, and left the houses standing still as they were.

So it growing towards night, and the tide almost spent, we hasted with our things down to the shallop, and got aboard that night, intending to have brought some beads and other things to have left in the houses, in sign of peace, and that we meant to truck with them; but it was not done by means of our hasty coming away from Cape Cod.[177] But so soon as we can meet conveniently with them, we will give them full satisfaction.[178] Thus much of our second discovery.

Having thus discovered this place, it was controversial[179] amongst us what to do touching our abode and settling there.[180]

Some thought it best, for many reasons, to abide there. As first, that there was a convenient harbor for boats, though not for ships. Secondly, good corn-ground ready to our hands, as we saw by experience in the goodly corn it yielded, which would again agree with the ground and be natural seed for the same. Thirdly, Cape Cod was like to be a place of good fishing; for we saw daily great whales, of the best kind for oil and bone, come close aboard our ship, and, in fair weather, swim and play about us.[181] There was once one, when the sun shone warm, came and lay above water, as if she had been dead, for a good while together, within half a musket shot of the ship; at which two were prepared to shoot, to see whether she would stir or no. He that gave fire first, his musket flew in pieces, both stock and barrel; yet, thanks, be to God, neither he nor any man else was hurt with it, though many were there about. But when the whale saw her time, she gave a snuff, and away. Fourthly, the place was likely to be healthful, secure, and defensible.

170. Gookin, in discussing Indian craft, particularly household goods and baskets, writes that "Many of them (are) very neat and artificial, with the portraitures of buds, beasts, fishes and flowers, upon them in colors."

171. In Massachusetts, these must have been deer's horns.

172. Dexter identifies the bird as probably the *Falco lencocephalus* or the *Falco Washingtonianus.* He also believes that it is possible that Bradford might have mistaken the huge fish hawk (*Falco haliaetus*) for an eagle.

173. Several seventeenth century writers have noted that the Indians dried acorns and by boiling them made an edible dish.

174. Dexter identifies (p. 36) this as *Aeschepias cornuti,* better known as milkweed or silkweed.

175. The Indians in New England planted a poor grade of tobacco.

176. Bullrush was evidently used for mats that were used to cover rough wigwams.

177. Dexter (pp. 37-38) believes that the Pilgrims intended to make another visit to these wigwams with beads, etc., for trading purposes but were prevented by their leaving for Plymouth shortly afterward and by the *Mayflower* leaving so early in the spring.

178. Bradford writes, "As about some six months afterwards they did, to their good content."

179. N. Morton uses the word *controverted.*

180. "That is, on the cleared land around Cornhill, and bordering Pamet River." (Dexter, p. 18)

181. See note 17. (p. 12)

MOURT'S
RELATION:
A JOURNAL
OF THE
PILGRIMS OF
PLYMOUTH

A RELATION OR
JOURNAL OF THE
PROCEEDINGS OF
THE PLANTATION
SETTLED AT
PLYMOUTH IN
NEW ENGLAND

But the last and especial reason was, that now the heart of winter and unseasonable weather was come upon us, so that we could not go upon coasting and discovery without danger of losing men and boat, upon which would follow the overthrow of all, especially considering what variable winds and sudden storms do there arise. Also, cold and wet lodging had so tainted our people, (for scarce any of us were free from vehement coughs,) as if they should continue long in that estate, it would endanger the lives of many, and breed diseases and infection amongst us. Again, we had yet some beer, butter, flesh, and other such victuals left, which would quickly be all gone; and then we should have nothing to comfort us in the great labor and toil we were likely to undergo at the first. It was also conceived, whilst we had competent victuals, that the ship would stay with us; but when that grew low, they would be gone, and let us shift as we could.[182]

Others, again, urged greatly the going to Anguum, or Angoum,[183] a place twenty leagues off to the northwards, which they had heard to be an excellent harbor for ships, better ground, and better fishing. Secondly, for any thing we knew, there might be hard by us a far better seat; and it should be a great hindrance to seat where[184] we should remove again. Thirdly, the water was but in ponds; and it was thought there would be none in summer, or very little. Fourthly, the water there must be fetched up a steep hill.[185]

But to omit many reasons and replies used hereabouts, it was in the end concluded to make some discovery within the bay; but in no case so far as Angoum.[186] Besides, Robert Coppin, our pilot,[187] made relation of a great navigable river[188] and good harbor in the other head-land of the bay,[189] almost right over against Cape Cod, being, in a right line, not much above eight leagues distant,[190] in which he had been once; and because that one of the wild men with whom they had some trucking stole a harping iron[191] from them, they called it *Thievish Harbor.* And beyond that place they were enjoined not to go. Whereupon a company was chosen to go[192] out upon a third discovery,[193] it pleased God that Mistress White was brought a bed of a

---

182. Dexter (p. 39) offers this as further evidence that the Pilgrims did not completely trust Jones.

183. Agawam, present day Ipswich on Cape Ann, north of Boston.

184. Young believes this to be an error for *whence,* while Dexter interprets it as "where they should be dissatisfied, and whence they should be therefore compelled to remove again."

185. At Cornhill, or on Old Tom's Hill, near the entrance of Pamet River.

186. Agawam.

187. The *Mayflower's* second mate. Dexter (p. 41) writes, "It is my impression that Coppin was originally hired to go in the *Speedwell;* that he was the 'pilot' whose 'coming' was a 'great encouragement' to the Leyden expectants in the last of May or first of June, 1620, that he sailed with them in the *Speedwell,* but, on her final putting back, was transferred to the *Mayflower* where Clarke . . . already was,—Robert Cushman having written to Leyden 11/21 June, 'We have *another* pilot here, one Mr. Clarke, who went last year to Virginia with a ship of kine.' "

188. Dexter (p. 41) states, "It is difficult to guess what suggested the idea of this 'great navigable river.' " Young suggests it is probably the North River in Scituate.

189. Manomet Point, directly south of the entrance to Plymouth harbor.

190. Dexter notes (p. 41) that "It would be a little less than 25 miles in an air line—one point south of due west—from the anchorage of the *Mayflower* in Provincetown harbor to her anchorage in Plymouth harbor."

191. A harpoon.

192. This expedition was to start out a week later.

193. The reference is to the second expedition which took place between November 27/December 7 and November 30/December 10.

son, which was called Peregrine.[194]

The fifth day we, through God's mercy, escaped a great danger by the foolishness of a boy, one of Francis Billington's sons,[195] who, in his father's absence, had got gunpowder, and had shot off a piece or two, and made squibs; and there being a fowling-piece charged in his father's cabin, shot her off in the cabin; there being a little barrel of powder half full, scattered in and about the cabin, the fire being within four foot of the bed between the decks, and many flints and iron things about the cabin, and many people about the fire; and yet, by God's mercy, no harm done.

Wednesday, the sixth of December.[196] It was resolved our discoverers should set forth, for the day before was too foul weather, — and so they did, though it was well o'er the day ere all things could be ready. So ten of our men were appointed who were of themselves willing to undertake it, to wit, Captain Standish, Master Carver,[197] William Bradford, Edward Winslow,[198] John Tilley, Edward Tilley,[199] John Howland,[200] and three of London,[201] Richard Warren,[202] Stephen Hopkins,[203]

194. Peregrine White, whose first name means *pilgrim,* was the son of William, a "woolcarder from England" and Susanna Fuller White. Mrs. White was the sister of Samuel Fuller, the physician. William White died February 21/March 3, 1620, leaving his widow and two sons, Resolved and Peregrine. Mrs. White married Edward Winslow on May 12/22, 1621, who raised the boys. He moved to Marshfield with his parents in 1632. He was an ensign, later lieutenant and captain, (1673) in Standish's militia. In 1648 he married Sarah Bassett and settled on an estate given him by his father-in-law William Bassett, between the North and South Rivers in Marshfield. In 1665 the General Court "granted unto him 200 acres of land, lying and being at the path that goes from Bridgewater to the Bay, adjoining to the Bay line." The grant was made "in respect that he was the first of the English that was born in these parts; and in answer unto his own petition preferred to this Court respecting the premises." He was a representative to the General Court in 1660 and 1673 and a member of the Council of War in the latter year. He had six children. Peregrine White died on July 20/31, 1704 nearly 84 years old "of a fever." *The Boston News-letter* (No. 15, July 31, 1704) noted that "He was vigorous and of a comely aspect to the last."

195. This should be *Francis,* one of *John* Billington's sons. He later discovered the lake still known as Billington's Sea. The date of the gunpowder experience noted above was December 5/15, 1620.

196. December 6/16, 1620.

197. John Carver, deacon of the Leyden congregation, was one of the agents sent to England to secure permission to found a colony in 1617. In the summer of 1620 he was in Southampton making arrangements for the *Mayflower* voyage. He was probably chosen governor at that time and re-elected in Provincetown harbor in November. He was elected again in March, made the treaty with Massasoit, and died soon afterward on April 5/15, 1621.

198. Edward Winslow, one of the authors of this writing, was one of the most distinguished members of this community. He was born at Droitwich, England, October 8/18, 1594, and joined the Leyden congregation about 1617. His wife Elizabeth Barker, whom he had married on May 16/26, 1618, died in the winter of 1620/1621, and he married Susanna Fuller White. (See note.) Always a leader in Plymouth Colony and close to William Bradford, he was chosen governor in 1633. He went to England several times on Colony business, was completely trusted as their agent, and merited their trust. He was one of Cromwell's commissioners in charge of the naval expedition to Hispaniola, died aboard ship May 8/18, 1654, and was buried at sea.

199. John Tilley, from the Leyden congregation, was a silk worker. He and his second wife, Bridget, died that first winter. His daughter Elizabeth married John Howland. Edward Tilley and his wife Ann also died that first winter.

200. John Howland, one of John Carver's men-servants, married Elizabeth Tilley (see note 199). He was Assistant, 1633-1635, frequently chosen Representative, and was generally a leader in the Colony's affairs. He died February 23/March 5, 1674. The *Plymouth Colony Records* say that "he was an ancient professor of the ways of Christ; one of the first comers, and proves a useful instrument of good."

201. The reference to "three of London" means that they were not members of John Robinson's congregation in Leyden.

202. Richard Warren, whom Bradford describes as "an useful instrument, and during his life bore a deep share in the difficulties and troubles of the first settlement of the plantation. He died in 1628.

203. See note 54. (p. 16)

MOURT'S
RELATION:
A JOURNAL
OF THE
PILGRIMS OF
PLYMOUTH

A RELATION OR
JOURNAL OF THE
PROCEEDINGS OF
THE PLANTATION
SETTLED AT
PLYMOUTH IN
NEW ENGLAND

and Edward Doten,[204] and two of our [205] seamen, John Alderton,[206] and Thomas English.[207] Of the ship's company there went two of the master's mates, Master Clarke[208] and Master Coppin, the master gunner, and three sailors.[209] The narration of which discovery follows, penned by one[210] of the company.

Wednesday, the sixth of December.[211] We set out, being very cold and hard weather. We were a long while, after we launched from the ship, before we could get clear of a sandy point, which lay within less than a furlong of the same.[212] In which time two were very sick, and Edward Tilley had like to have sounded[213] with cold. The gunner also was sick unto death (but hope of trucking made him to go,) and so remained all that day and the next night. At length we got clear of the sandy point, and got up our sails, and within an hour or two we got under the weather shore,[214] and then had smoother water and better sailing. But it was very cold; for the water froze on our clothes, and made them many times like coats of iron.

We sailed six or seven leagues by the shore, but saw neither river nor creek. At length we met with a tongue of land, being flat off from the shore, with a sandy point.[215] We bore up to gain the point, and found there a fair income or road of a bay, being a league over at the narrowest, and some two or three in length; but we made right over to the land before us, and left the discovery of this income till the next day.[216] As we drew near to the shore,[217] we espied some ten or twelve Indians very busy about a black thing,—what it was we could not tell,—till afterwards they saw us, and ran to and fro, as if they had been carrying something away. We landed a league or two from them, and had much ado to put ashore any where, it lay so full of flat sands.[218] When we came to shore, we made us a barricado, and got firewood,

---

204. Edward Doten, who was a servant of Stephen Hopkins, was one of the purchasers of Dartmouth and later moved to Yarmouth, where he died August 23/September 2, 1655.

205. Young explains, "They were not a part of the *Mayflower's* crew, but were intended to remain in the country and to manage the *Speedwell,* had she come over. Their occupation at present, I suppose, was to take charge of the shallop, until another small vessel should be sent over; which took place in August 1623, when a pinnace of 44 tons, called the *Little James,* arrived."

206. John Alderton, "being a seaman," came over as one of the company but "was to go back . . . for the help of others behind." He died that first winter. (Bradford's account)

207. Thomas English was hired as "master of a shallop here," but he, like John Allerton, "died before the ship returned."

208. *Master Clarke,* the master's mate and pilot of the *Mayflower,* who had been to Virginia in 1619; Clark's Island in Plymouth harbor is named in his honor, for he is reported to have been the first to land on the island.

209. The names of the sailors are, of course, unknown. There were eighteen members of this party.

210. Either Bradford or Winslow. All of the internal evidence would seem to indicate that Bradford wrote this portion.

211. December 6/16, 1620.

212. Freeman says this is the "end of Long Point," and Dexter adds, "A northeaster was evidently blowing, and they could not lie close enough into the wind to clear this point with sails, and probably the wind and incoming tide together, made it hard for them to row their shallop around it." (p. 46)

213. Swooned.

214. That is the shore of Truro where, according to Dexter (p. 46), "as they came near the land they would gain some protection from the roughness both of the wind and sea."

215. Billingsgate Point. In Young's description, "This point then joined the land north of it; but is now an island, having been cut off by a ditch many years since." (p. 151)

216. This *income* is the *cul de sac* of Wellfleet Bay.

217. In Eastham, a little north of Great Pond.

218. Young writes (p. 152), probably borrowing from Freeman's *Cape Cod,* "A sandy flat, a mile wide, extends along the western shore of Eastham, from Dennis to the bounds of Wellfleet. It is left dry about three hours, and may easily be crossed by horses and carriages."

and set out sentinels, and betook us to our lodging, such as it was. We saw the smoke of the fire which the savages made that night about four or five miles from us.

In the morning,[219] we divided our company, some eight in the shallop, and the rest on the shore went to discover this place.[220] But we found it only to be a bay, without either river or creek coming into it. Yet we deemed it to be as good a harbor as Cape Cod; for they that sounded it found a ship might ride in five fathom water. We on the land found it to be a level[221] soil, though none of the fruitfullest. We saw two becks[222] of fresh water, which were the first running streams that we saw in the country; but one might stride over them. We found also a great fish, called a grampus,[223] dead on the sands. They in the shallop found two of them also in the bottom of the bay, dead in like sort. They were cast up at high water, and could not get off for the frost and ice. They were some five or six paces long, and about two inches thick of fat, and fleshed like a swine. They would have yielded a great deal of oil, if there had been time and means to have taken it. So we finding nothing for our turn, both we and our shallop returned.

We then directed our course along the sea sands to the place where we first saw the Indians.[224] When we were there, we saw it was also a grampus which they were cutting up. They cut it into long rands[225] or pieces, about an ell[226] long and two handfull broad. We found here and there a piece scattered by the way, as it seemed for haste. This place the most were minded we should call the *Grampus Bay,*[227] because we found so many of them there. We followed the track of the Indian's bare feet a good way on the sands. At length we saw where they struck into the woods by the side of a pond.[228] As we went to view the place, one said he thought he saw an Indian house among the trees; so we went up to see. And here we and the shallop lost sight one of another till night, it being now about nine or ten o'clock. So we light on a path, but saw no house, and followed a great way into the woods.[229] At length we found where corn had been set, but not that year. Anon, we found a great burying place, one part whereof was encompassed with a large palisado, like a churchyard, with young spires,[230] four or five yards long, set as close one by another as they

MOURT'S RELATION: A JOURNAL OF THE PILGRIMS OF PLYMOUTH

A RELATION OR JOURNAL OF THE PROCEEDINGS OF THE PLANTATION SETTLED AT PLYMOUTH IN NEW ENGLAND

---

219. Thursday, December 7/17, 1620.

220. The *income* of Wellfleet bay which Young describes as "large, indented within with creeks, where vessels of 70 or 80 tons may lie."

221. "The land in Eastham is a level plain." (Young, p. 152)

222. Beck—a small river or brook. Young writes (p. 152), "One of these no doubt was Indian brook, which forms the boundary between Eastham and Wellfleet and runs into the harbor of Silver Springs. The spring from which it issues has a white sand at the bottom resembling that metal. The other was probably Cook's brook, in Eastham, three quarters of a mile south of Indian brook, or possibly Snow's brook, a mile further south."

223. Young's description (p. 152) of the grampus follows: "The grampus . . . is the largest and most remarkable species of the genus *Phocaena* of the cetaceous order of Mammalia. It is a large animal, half the size of the Greenland full-grown whale, being often seen from 25 to 30 feet in length, and 10 or 12 in circumference. The color is black above suddenly giving place to white on the sides, which is continued over the abdomen. Individuals of this species are sometimes thrown ashore on the Cape, 20 feet long, and having four inches of blubber."

224. They went back, north, towards Wellfleet harbor.

225. Rands = strips, usually of beef.

226. Forty-five inches.

227. Wellfleet harbor.

228. Freeman indicates that this was "Great pond, in Eastham, north of which they landed," and Young adds that "This pond is a quarter of a mile from shore. A narrow neck, about forty feet wide, separates it from Long Pond."

229. Dexter suggest that this was probably "in the direction of Enoch's Rock and Nauset light."

230. Young (p. 154) defines spires as "twisted or wreathed boughs," and Dexter calls them "shoots or young saplings."

MOURT'S
RELATION:
A JOURNAL
OF THE
PILGRIMS
OF
PLYMOUTH

A RELATION OR
JOURNAL OF THE
PROCEEDINGS OF
THE PLANTATION
SETTLED AT
PLYMOUTH IN
NEW ENGLAND

could, two or three foot in the ground. Within it was full of graves, some bigger and some less. Some were also paled about; and others had like an Indian house[231] made over them, but not matted. Those graves were more sumptuous than those at *Cornhill;* yet we digged none of them up, but only viewed them and went our way. Without the palisado were graves also, but not so costly. From this place we went and found more corn-ground, but not of this year. As we ranged, we light on four or five Indian houses, which had been lately dwelt in; but they were uncovered, and had no mats about them; else they were like those we found at *Cornhill,* but had not been so lately dwelt in. There was nothing left but two or three peices of oil mats, and a little sedge. Also, a little further, we found two baskets full of parched acorns,[232] hid in the ground, which we supposed had been corn when we began to dig the same; we cast earth thereon again, and went our way. All this while we saw no people.

We went ranging up and down till the sun began to draw low, and then we hasted out of the woods, that we might come to our shallop; which, when we were out of the woods, we espied a great way off, and called them to come unto us; the which they did as soon as they could, for it was not yet high water.[233] They were exceeding glad to see us, for they feared because they had not seen us in so long a time, thinking we would have kept by the shore side. So being both weary and faint, — for we had eaten nothing all that day, — we fell to make our rendezvous[234] and get firewood, which always costs us a great deal of labor.[235] By that time we had done, and our shallop come to us,[236] it was within night; and we fed upon such victuals as we had, and betook us to rest, after we had set out our watch. About midnight we heard a great and hideous cry; and our sentinels called, *"Arm! Arm!"* So we bestirred ourselves and shot off a couple of muskets, and the noise ceased. We concluded that it was a company of wolves or foxes; for one[237] told us he had heard such a noise in Newfoundland.[238]

About five o'clock in the morning[239] we began to be stirring; and two or three, which doubted whether their pieces would go off or no, made trial of them and shot them off, but thought nothing at all. After prayer[240] we prepared ourselves for

---

231. Thomas Morton (Ch. 17) writes "Over the grave of the more noble they erect something in the form of a hearse cloth."

232. According to Roger Williams the Indians boiled dried acorns when corn was scarce.

233. Bradford writes *(Of Plimoth Plantation),* "When the sun grew low, they hasted out of the woods to meet with their shallop, to whom they made signs to come to them into a creek hard by, the which they did at high water; of which they were very glad, for they had not seen each other all that day, since the morning."

234. N. Morton suggests that this creek is the Namskiket, which divides Orleans from Brewster, but Dexter offers good evidence (p. 50-1) that "the first creek which they would come to in their wasting southwestwardly is that here referred to, *viz.,* Great Meadow Creek (or Herring River) in Eastham, one mile n.n.e. of Rock Harbor." Young supports Dexter's view. (p. 155)

235. Dexter reasons (p. 51) that "The trees were lofty, and the undergrowth was annually burned by the Indians, so that they doubtless found it difficult to gather wood suitable for their fire without felling large timber; which, with their tools, would be a slow and difficult task."

236. See note 233, above.

237. Bradford writes that "one of the seamen told them that he had often heard such a noise in Newfoundland." Young (p. 155) suggests that either Coppin or Clarke who had visited the coast earlier, were the informants, but Dexter believes that Bradford's statement referred to one of the "three sailors who accompanied the party."

238. From the 1580's on, many British vessels had visited Newfoundland, which Sir Humphry Gilbert had claimed for Queen Elizabeth in 1586.

239. Friday, December 8/18, 1620.

240. Young points out (p. 156) that "This incidental remark shows the religious character of the Pilgrims. No dangers or hardships were permitted to interfere with their stated devotions."

MOURT'S
RELATION:
A JOURNAL
OF THE
PILGRIMS OF
PLYMOUTH

A RELATION OR
JOURNAL OF THE
PROCEEDINGS OF
THE PLANTATION
SETTLED AT
PLYMOUTH IN
NEW ENGLAND

breakfast, and for a journey; and it being now the twilight in the morning, it was thought meet to carry the things down to the shallop. Some said it was not best to carry the armor[241] down. Others said, they would be readier. Two or three said they would not carry theirs till they went themselves, but mistrusting nothing at all. As it fell out, the water not being high enough, they laid the things down upon the shore, and came up to breakfast. Anon, all upon a sudden, we heard a great and strange cry, which we knew to be the same voices, though they varied their notes. One of our company, being aboard, came running in, and cried, "They are men! Indians! Indians!" and withal their arrows came flying amongst us. Our men ran out with all speed to recover their arms; as by the good providence of God they did. In the mean time, Captain Miles Standish, having a snaphance[242] ready, made a shot; and after him another. After they two had shot, other two of us were ready; but he wished us not to shoot till we could take aim, for we knew not what need we should have; and there were four only of us which had their arms there ready,[243] and stood before the open side of our barricado, which was first assaulted. They thought it best to defend it, lest the enemy should take it and our stuff; and so have the more vantage against us. Our care was no less for the shallop; but we hoped all the rest would defend it. We called unto them to know how it was with them; and they answered "Well! Well!" every one, and "Be of good courage!" We heard three of their pieces go off, and the rest called for a firebrand to light their matches.[244] One[245] took a log out of the fire on his shoulder and went and carried it unto them; which was thought did not little discourage our enemies. The cry of our enemies was dreadful, especially when our men ran out to recover their arms. Their note was after this manner, *"Woach, woach, ha ha hach woach."*[246] Our men were no sooner come to their arms, but the enemy was ready to assault them.

There was a lusty man, and no whit less valiant, who was thought to be their captain, stood behind a tree within half a musket shot of us, and there let his arrows fly at us. He was seen to shoot three arrows, which were all avoided; for he at whom the first arrow was aimed, saw it, and stooped down, and it flew over him. The rest were avoided also. He stood three shots of a musket. At length, one took, as he said, full aim at him; after which he gave an extraordinary cry, and away they went all.[247]

---

241. They evidently wore coats of mail on all of these excursions.

242. Young (p. 156) defines a *snaphance* as "a musket with a flintlock." Dexter (p. 52) indicates that this gun "appears to have been the result of the first rude contrivance to fire a gun without 'touching it off,' like a cannon, with a match; preceding by some years the 'flint-lock.' It was invented by the Dutch, and struck fire with a flint, but in a different, clumsier, and more uncertain way than the flint-lock, which was not introduced until Queen Elizabeth's time." Young (p. 157) distinguishes between a firelock and a snaphance in pointing out that in the latter, "a moveable hammer was placed beyond the pan, and separated from its cover; whilst in the firelock the hammer is affixed to the pan, supplying the place of its cover, and opening at the percussion of the cork."

243. "That is, had lighted their gunmatch from the fire, and so made ready for a discharge." (Mourt, p. 52)

244. Further proving that they were using matchlocks.

245. Evidently one of the four who were at the barricado.

246. Obviously, these sounds cannot be translated. They probably represent the best memory that Bradford had of the event.

247. Both Young (p. 158) and Dexter (pp. 53-54) repeat the account by Johnson in his *Wonderworking Providence*, Ch. 8, printed in 1654, that "our Captain Miles Standish, having his fowling-piece in readiness, presented full at them. His shot, being directed by the provident hand of the most high God, struck the stoutest sachem among them on the right arm, it being bent over his shoulder to reach an arrow forth his quiver, as their manner is to draw them forth in fight. At this stroke they all fled with great swiftness through the woods and thickets. Then the English, who more thirsted after their conversion than destruction, returned to their boat without receiving any damage." No other writer tells this story, and Bradford in writing the account for his *Of Plimoth Plantation* reiterates the story that he tells in this *Relation.*

MOURT'S
RELATION:
A JOURNAL
OF THE
PILGRIMS OF
PLYMOUTH

A RELATION OR
JOURNAL OF THE
PROCEEDINGS OF
THE PLANTATION
SETTLED AT
PLYMOUTH IN
NEW ENGLAND

We followed them about a quarter of a mile; but we left six to keep our shallop, for we were very careful of our business. Then we shouted all together two several times, and shot off a couple of muskets, and so returned. This we did that they might see we were not afraid of them, nor discouraged.

Thus it pleased God to vanquish our enemies[248] and give us deliverance. By their noise we could not guess that they were less than thirty or forty, though some thought that they were many more. Yet, in the dark of the morning, we could not so well discern them among the trees, as they could see us by our fire-side. We took up eighteen of their arrows, which we have sent to England by Master Jones;[249] some whereof were headed with brass, others with harts' horn, and others with eagles' claws.[250] Many more no doubt were shot, for these we found were almost covered with leaves;[251] yet, by the especial providence of God, none of them either hit or hurt us, though many came close by us and on every side of us, and some coats which hung up in our barricado were shot through and through.

So after we had given God thanks for our deliverance, we took our shallop and went on our journey, and called this place *The First Encounter*. From hence we intended to have sailed to the aforesaid *Thievish Harbor*,[252] if we found no convenient harbor by the way. Having the wind good, we sailed all that day along the coast about fifteen leagues;[253] but saw neither river nor creek[254] to put into. After we had sailed an hour or two, it began to snow and rain, and to be bad weather.[255] About the midst of the afternoon the wind increased, and the seas began to be very rough; and the hinges of the rudder broke, so that we could steer no longer with it, but two men, with much ado, were fain to serve with a couple of oars. The seas were grown so great that we were much troubled and in great danger; and night grew on. Anon, Master Coppin bade us be of good cheer; he saw the harbor.[256] As we drew near, the gale being stiff, and we bearing great sail to get in, split our mast in three pieces,

---

248. These were Nauset Indians. Samoset later informed the Pilgrims "that their hostility was occasioned by the fact that one 'Hunt' had previously deceived them, and stolen some of their tribe and sold them for slaves." (Dexter, p. 54)

249. When the *Mayflower* returned in April, 1621.

250. Dexter notes, "No mention is here made of what seems to have been the commonest arrow-heads of the Indians, viz., flint; doubtless because the Indians on the Cape were not favorably situated for procuring them." (p. 55)

251. This meaning of this clause is somewhat obscure. Dexter states, "The only sense which I can afford to these words is to suppose that they found the arrows which they picked up had transfixed and strung many leaves upon themselves in their flight through the thick trees, where the dried leaves still clung to the branches." (p. 55)

252. Plymouth.

253. Dexter reasons (p. 56) that "They coasted along within sight of the shore all the way, so as to discover, if possible, some harbor, into which they might go. This coasting, from the place of their 'first encounter' in Eastham, to Manomet Bluff, which marks the southern side of Plymouth Bay, would be fifteen leagues, good measure." Young (p. 159) agrees with this.

254. They missed several small creeks along the way.

255. Young notes (p. 159) that "The snow-storm, which began 'after they had sailed an hour or two,' prevented their seeing Sandy Neck, and led them to overshoot Barnstable harbor. Had it not been for this, it is highly probable that they would have entered and made their settlement there." Dexter (p. 56) agrees with this, and he adds, that the snowstorm was "still a blessing, in preventing them from settling (as they might have done had they gone in there) in a much less favorable place than Plymouth."

256. Dexter believes (p. 56) that "He probably recognized Manomet looming through the storm, and after passing Manomet Point steered n.w. by Elisha's Point to shoot in."

and were like to have cast away our shallop.[257] Yet, by God's mercy, recovering our-selves, we had the flood with us, and struck into the harbor.

Now he that thought that had been the place was deceived, it being a place where not any of us had been before; and coming into the harbor, he that was our pilot did bear up northward,[258] which if we had continued, we had been cast away.[259] Yet still the Lord kept us, and we bare up for an island[260] before us; and recovering of that island, being compassed about with many rocks, and dark night growing upon us, it pleased the Divine Providence that we fell upon a place of sandy ground, where our shallop did ride safe and secure all that night; and coming upon a strange island, kept our watch all night in the rain upon that island.[261] And in the morning[262] we marched about it, and found no inhabitants at all; and here we made our rendezvous all that day, being Saturday.

10th[263] of December. On the Sabbath day we rested; and on Monday[264] we sounded the harbor, and found it a very good harbor for our shipping. We marched also into the land,[265] and found divers cornfields, and little running brooks,[266] a place very good for situation. So we returned to our ship[267] again with good news to the rest of our people, which did much comfort their hearts.[268]

257. Bradford retells the story in his *Of Plimoth Plantation:* "Yet by God's mercy they recovered themselves, and having the flood with them, struck into the harbor. But when it came to, the pilot was deceived in the places, and said the Lord be merciful unto them for his eyes never saw that place before; and he and the master's mate would have run her ashore in a cove full of breakers before the wind. But a lusty seaman which steered bade those which rowed, if they were men, about with her or else they were all cast away; the which they did with speed. So he bid them be of good cheer and row lustily, for there was a fair sound before them, and he doubted not but they should find one place or other where they might ride in safety. And though it was very dark and rained sore, yet in the end they got under the lee of a small island and remained there all that night in safety."

258. See previous note.

259. The cove was between the Gurnet Head and Saquish Point at the entrance of Plymouth harbor.

260. Clark's Island in the entrance of Plymouth harbor is named for the mate of the *Mayflower,* the first person to land there.

261. Friday, December 8/18, 1620.

262. Saturday, December 9/19, 1620.

263. Sunday, December 10/10, 1620. This was the first religious service celebrated on land by the Pilgrims.

264. Monday, December 11/21, 1620, the day still celebrated as Forefathers' Day.

265. The exact place of the landing is not absolutely certain, but popular "tradition had declared that it was on a large rock at the foot of a cliff near the termination of the north street leading to the water." (Young, p. 161) This editor does not intend to become involved in the Plymouth Rock controversy in this work.

266. Dexter (p. 59) points out that there are eight brooks running into the harbor Eel River, Wellingsley, Town Brook, and five rivulets toward Jones River.

267. Young points out that "They left the *Mayflower* in Cape Cod harbor, December 6, and were three days in getting to Plymouth. They probably started on their return to the ship on the 13th, and striking across the bay a distance of 25 miles, reached her on the 14th."

268. The day after the party left the vessel (December 7/17, 1620). Dorothy Bradford, wife of William Bradford, who was one of the party, fell overboard and was drowned.

A Relation or Journal of the Proceedings of the Plantation Settled at Plymouth in New England

(II)

On the 15th day[1] we weighed anchor to go to the place we had discovered; and coming within two leagues of the land, we could not fetch the harbor, but were fain to put round[2] again towards Cape Cod, our course lying west, and the wind was at northwest. But it pleased God that the next day, being Saturday the 16th day, the wind came fair, and we put to sea again, and came safely into a safe harbor; and within half an hour the wind changed, so as if we had been letted[3] but a little, we had gone back to Cape Cod.

This harbor is a bay greater than Cape Cod, compassed with a goodly land; and in the bay two fine islands,[4] uninhabited, wherein are nothing but woods, oaks, pines, walnuts, beech, sassafras, vines, and other trees[5] which we know not. This bay is a most hopeful place; innumerable store of fowl, and excellent good; and cannot but be of fish in their seasons; skate,[6] cod, turbot,[7] and herring,[8] we have tasted of; abundance of mussels, the greatest and best that ever we saw; crabs and

---

1. Friday, December 15/25, 1620.

2. In the original printing the word is *roome*, obviously a printer's error.

3. Letted = hindered.

4. Clark's Island is now the only island in Plymouth harbor. Dexter conjectures that Saquish might have been conceived an island, "if the sea then flowed across the neck connecting it with Gurnet Head, as is not improbable." (p. 60) Young (p. 162) supposes "that a shoal, called Brown's Island, which lies near the entrance of the harbor, about half a mile east by north of Beach point, was above water at the time the Pilgrims arrived."

5. None of the forest trees of that period are found on Clark's Island or Saquish.

6. In the original printing the word is *Skote,* obviously a misspelling. The skate *(Raia bates)* for many years was caught off Plymouth.

7. Dexter (p. 60) indicates that the turbot *(Rhombus maximus)* is not found in these waters. He believes the fish indicated is probably the flounder *(Platessa plana),* which was plentiful off the New England coast.

8. The herring or alewive, the *Clupea elongata* and *Alosa vernalis,* were plentiful in all of this area through the nineteenth century.

MOURT'S
RELATION:
A JOURNAL
OF THE
PILGRIMS OF
PLYMOUTH

A RELATION OR
JOURNAL OF THE
PROCEEDINGS OF
THE PLANTATION
SETTLED AT
PLYMOUTH IN
NEW ENGLAND

lobsters,[9] in their time, infinite. It is in fashion like a sickle, or fish-hook.[10]

Monday, the 18th day.[11] We went a land,[12] manned with the master of the ship and three or four of the sailors. We marched along the coast in the woods some seven or eight miles,[13] but saw not an Indian nor an Indian house; only we found where they had planted their corn. We found not any navigable river, but four or five small running brooks[14] of very sweet fresh water, that all run into the sea. The land for the crust of the earth is a spit's depth,[15] excellent black mould, and fat in some places,[16] two or three great oaks, but not very thick, pines, walnuts, beech,[17] ash, birch, hazel,[18] holly, asp,[19] sassafras in abundance, and vines everywhere, cherry trees,[20] plum trees,[21] and many others which we know not.[22] Many kinds of herbs we found here in winter, as strawberry leaves innumerable, sorrel,[23] yarrow,[24] chervil,[25] brooklime,[26] liverwort,[27] watercresses,[28] great store of leeks and onions,[29] and an excellent strong kind of flax and hemp.[30] Here is sand, gravel, and excellent clay, no better in the world,[31] excellent for pots, and will wash like soap, and great store of stone,[32] though somewhat soft, and the best water[33] that ever we drunk; and the

---

9. Crabs, lobsters, and mussels are still found in the Plymouth area.

10. This is a description of Plymouth Bay including the harbors of Kingston and Duxbury.

11. Monday, December 18/28, 1620. In the original printing (1622) the date is given as "Monday the 13 day" which Dexter reprints without comment. Young (p. 164) correctly identifies the day as "the 18th day."

12. Young believes the words "in the long-boat" should be inserted at this point. (p. 164)

13. Both Young (p. 165) and Dexter (p. 61) agree that this is an exaggeration. Freeman indicates that "Which ever way the travelers went, they could not have walked seven miles; because northwest, at the distance of four miles, they would have come to Jones's River in Kingston, and southeast, at the distance of three miles, to Eel River. These rivers, though not large, cannot be denominated brooks."

14. Young identifies these brooks north of the village as Wellingsley Brook, Double Brook or Shingle Brook, Beaver Sam Brook, and Indian Brook.

15. A spade's depth.

16. Young notes, "This is an exact description of a strip of land, between the hills and the sea-shore, where the gardens now (1841) are. The soil too is good on Clark's Island, Saquish, and the Gurnet.

17. The beech or *Fagus Sylvatica* still grows in the area, "a clean, beautiful tree."

18. The *Corylus Americana*.

19. Dexter (p. 62) and Young (p. 165) identify this as the American Aspen (*Populus tremuliformis*).

20. Dexter notes, "Perhaps the northern red cherry (*Cerasus Pennsylvanica*) may have grown there; the black cherry (*Cerasus serotina*) and choke-cherry (*Cerasus Virginiana*) certainly did." (p. 62)

21. Dexter (p. 62) indicates these are "*Prunus maritima* and possibly also *Prunus Americana*." The plum tree is rarely cultivated in this area now.

22. There are still a great many varieties of trees in southeastern Massachusetts.

23. *Sorrell* is *Rumex acetosella*. There are many types of sorrel. The sour fleshy leaves of this plant are used in salads.

24. Yarrow is *Achillen millefolium*. This herb has a distinctive smell and taste, finely divided leaves, and small white or pink flowers.

25. In the original edition this is written carvel. Chervil (*Chaerophyllum sativum*) is a plant of the carrot family with fine leaves. The leaves are used for flavoring soups and salads and garnishing meat.

26. *Brooklime (Veronica baccabunga)*. Veronicas generally grow in wet places.

27. *Liverwort (Hepatica triloba)* is a type of bryophyte.

28. *Watercress = Nasturtum palustre* or *cardamine hirsuta*.

29. Dexter (p. 62) identifies them as *Allium tricoccum* and *Allium Canadeuse*.

30. Dexter identifies the hemp as *Linum Virginianum* and perhaps *Apocynum cannabinum*.

31. There is an abundance of clay in southeastern Massachusetts, and the manufacture of bricks and chimney linings has long been a prosperous business there.

32. There is still plenty of sand, gravel, and clay, but Young points out that "there is not much stone at Plymouth; a few bowlders (sic) of sienite."

33. Freeman writes that "Plymouth is abundantly supplied with springs and brooks of excellent water."

MOURT'S
RELATION:
A JOURNAL
OF THE
PILGRIMS OF
PLYMOUTH

A RELATION OR
JOURNAL OF THE
PROCEEDINGS OF
THE PLANTATION
SETTLED AT
PLYMOUTH IN
NEW ENGLAND

brooks now begin to be full of fish.[34] That night, many being weary with marching, we went aboard again.

The next morning, being Tuesday,[35] the 19th of December, we went again to discover further; some went on land, and some in the shallop. The land we found as the former day we did; and we found a creek, and went up three English miles, a very pleasant river[36] at full sea. A bark of thirty tons may go up; but at low water scarce our shallop could pass. This place[37] we had a great liking to plant in, but that it was so far from our fishing, our principal profit, and so encompassed with woods, that we should be in much danger of the savages; and our number being so little, and so much ground to clear; so as we thought good to quit and[38] clear that place till we were of more strength. Some of us, having a good mind, for safety, to plant in the greater isle,[39] we crossed the bay, which is there five or six miles over,[40] and found the isle about a mile and a half or two miles about,[41] all wooded, and no fresh water but two or three pits, that we doubted of fresh water in summer, and so full of wood as we could hardly clear so much as to serve us for corn. Besides, we judged it cold for our corn, and some part very rocky; yet divers thought of it as a place defensible, and a great security. That night we returned again a shipboard, with resolution the next morning to settle on some of those places.

So in the morning,[42] after we had called on God for direction, we came to this resolution, to go presently ashore again, and to take a better view of two places which we thought most fitting for us; for we could not now take time for further search or consideration, our victuals being much spent, especially our beer, and it being now the 19th of December. After our landing and viewing of the places, so well as we could, we came to a conclusion, by most voices, to set on the main land, on the first place, on a high ground,[43] where there is a great deal of land cleared, and hath been planted with corn three or four years ago; and there is a very sweet brook[44] runs under the hill side, and many delicate springs of as good water as can be drunk, and where we may harbor our shallops and boats exceeding well; and in this brook much good fish in their seasons; on the further side of the river also much corn-ground cleared.[45] In one field is a great hill,[46] on which we point to make a platform,

---

34. Young writes (p. 166) that "Some years since, before the Town Brook was obstructed, tomcods were abundant in December; eels and smelt enter the brooks in autumn." The tomcod is a small saltwater food fish resembling the cod.

35. Tuesday, December 19/29, 1620.

36. Jones River in Kingston.

37. The village of Kingston.

38. Young (p. 167) believes that the word *not* is accidentally omitted here. Dexter (p. 63) disagrees, asserting that *clear* is used to mean leave or pass away from.

39. Clarks' Island.

40. The distance from the mouth of Jones River across the bay to the Gurnet is five miles; from the mouth of the river to Clark's Island is less than four miles.

41. An accurate description.

42. Wednesday, December 20/30, 1620.

43. "On the bank, facing the harbor." (Young, p. 167)

44. According to Freeman, "Now called Town brook. It issues from a pond called Billington Sea." Dexter states, "This description indicates that they pitched upon the high land below Burian Hill, and just N.W. of Town Brook." (p. 64)

45. "On the spot now called the Training Green." (Young, p. 168)

46. "The Burial Hill, rising 165 feet above the level of the sea, and covering about eight acres." (Young, p. 168) Dexter adds, "A rude fort was early built on the S.W. summit, and in 1675, in Phillip's War, a strong stockade was erected there. It commands a most charming view of the town, the harbor, and the neighborhood." (Dexter, p. 65)

MOURT'S
RELATION:
A JOURNAL
OF THE
PILGRIMS OF
PLYMOUTH

A RELATION OR
JOURNAL OF THE
PROCEEDINGS OF
THE PLANTATION
SETTLED AT
PLYMOUTH IN
NEW ENGLAND

and plant our ordnance, which will command all round about. From thence we may see into the bay, and far into the sea; and we may see thence Cape Cod.[47] Our greatest labor will be fetching of our wood, which is half a quarter of an English mile; but there is enough so far off. What people inhabit here we yet know not, for as yet we have seen none. So there we made our rendezvous, and a place for some of our people, about twenty, resolving in the morning to come all ashore and to build houses.

But the next morning, being Thursday, the 21st of December, it was stormy and wet, that we could not go ashore; and those that remained there all night could do nothing, but were wet, not having daylight enough to make them a sufficient court of guard,[48] to keep them dry. All that night it blew and rained extremely. It was so tempestuous that the shallop could not go on land so soon as was meet, for they had no victuals on land. About eleven o'clock, the shallop went off with much ado with provision, but could not return, it blew so strong; and was such foul weather that we were forced to let fall our anchor, and ride with three anchors ahead.[49]

Friday, the 22d, the storm still continued, that we could not get a land, nor they come to us aboard. This morning Goodwife Allerton,[50] was delivered of a son, but dead born.

Saturday, the 23d, so many of us as could went on shore, felled and carried timber, to provide themselves stuff for building.

Sunday, the 24th, our people on shore heard a cry of some savages, as they thought, which caused an alarm and to stand on their guard, expecting an assault; but all was quiet.[51]

Monday, the 25th day, we went on shore, some to fell timber, some to saw, some to rive, and some to carry;[52] so no man rested all that day.[53] But, towards night, some, as they were at work, heard a noise of some Indians, which caused us all to go to our muskets; but we heard no further. So we came aboard again, and left some twenty to keep the court of guard. That night we had a sore storm of wind and rain.

Monday, the 25th, being Christmas Day, we began to drink water aboard. But at night the master caused us to have some beer;[54] and so on board we had divers times now and then some beer, but on shore none at all.

Tuesday, the 26th, it was foul weather, that we could not go ashore.[55]

Wednesday, the 27th, we went to work again.[56]

Thursday, the 28th of December,[57] so many as could went to work on the hill, where we purposed to build our platform for our ordnance,[58] and which doth com-

---

47. On a clear day this can still be done.

48. *Cour de garde,* a guardhouse.

49. Bradford notes, "December 21, dies Richard Britterige, the first who dies in this harbor." (Prince, p. 168)

50. This child, the second born among the Pilgrims in New England, was the son of Isaac and Mary Allerton.

51. December 24. (January 3, 1621, n.s.) "And this day dies Solomon Martin, the sixth and last who dies this month." (Bradford in Prince, p. 168) Young (p. 169) believes Solomon to be Christopher Martin's son, but "Solomon Martin" was undoubtedly Solomon Prower, Martin's servant.

52. Bradford adds, "And the 25th day began to erect the first house for common use to receive them and their goods." *(Of Plimoth Plantation).*

53. About twenty were kept on guard on shore, and the rest returned to the ship.

54. Dexter notes that the "stock was getting low and necessitated scant allowance." (p. 24)

55. December 26, 1620/January 5, 1621.

56. December 27, 1620/January 6, 1621.

57. December 28; 1620/January 7, 1621.

58. Young in 1841 pointed out that "vestiges of this fortification are still visible on the Burial hill." (p. 170)

MOURT'S
RELATION:
A JOURNAL
OF THE
PILGRIMS OF
PLYMOUTH

A RELATION OR
JOURNAL OF THE
PROCEEDINGS OF
THE PLANTATION
SETTLED AT
PLYMOUTH IN
NEW ENGLAND

mand all the plain and the bay, and from whence we may see far into the sea,[59] and might be easier impaled, having two rows of houses and a fair street.[60] So in the afternoon we went to measure out the grounds, and first we took notice how many families there were, willing all single men that had no wives to join with some family, as they thought fit, that so we might build fewer houses; which was done, and we reduced them to nineteen families.[61] To greater families we allotted larger plots;[62] to every person half a pole in breadth, and three in length,[63] and so lots were cast where every man should lie; which was done, and staked out. We thought this proportion was large enough at the first, for houses and gardens to impale them round,[64] considering the weakness of our people, many of them growing ill with colds; for our former discoveries in frost and storms, and the wading at Cape Cod had brought much weakness amongst us, which increased so every day more and more, and after was the cause of many of their deaths.

Friday and Saturday[65] we fitted ourselves for our labor; but our people on shore were much troubled and discouraged with rain and wet that day, being very stormy and cold. We saw great smokes of fire[66] made by the Indians, about six or seven miles from us, as we conjectured.[67]

Monday, the 1st of January, we went betimes to work. We were much hindered in lying so far off from the land, and fain to go as the tide served, that we lost much time; for our ship drew so much water[68] that she lay a mile and almost a half off, though a ship of seventy or eighty tons at high water may come to the shore.[69]

Wednesday, the third of January,[70] some of our people being abroad to get and

59. Young writes, "I think there is something omitted here. The house-lots were not laid out on the hill, but in front of it, on Leyden-street, which runs from the Town Square to Water-street." (p. 170) Dexter remarks that Young "took their language as implying that they now commenced to build their stockade on the summit of Burial Hill, and so could not connect the 'two rows of houses and a fair street' with that. It seems to me, however, that their language only implies that they commenced work on the slope of the hill, on the summit of which they intended by and by to build their 'platform for ordnance,' and that they proceeded to lay out on that slope the first street, and the first lots, and to assign them to families and groups; this need being more pressing than the other. The common house was now (rudely) complete, as their temporary shelter (with the ship) while building their several dwellings, and the time had come for the latter work." (p. 67)

60. Leyden Street.

61. Dexter points out that, "When they reached Cape Cod, there were eighteen husbands and wives in the company — besides four fathers, each with one or more sons; as the basis of this classification into families." (p. 68)

62. Carver's lot, for example, since there were eight in his family group, would be 66 feet (4 poles) front and 49½ feet depth.

63. A pole is 16½ feet so that each person's grant of land was 8½ feet front by 49½ feet depth.

64. Dexter explains, "These grounds were measured out on the north and south sides of what is now Leyden Street. The first volume of the Plymouth Records of Deeds contains, in Gov. Bradford's handwriting, a rude plot of this street, with the names of seven of those whose lots fell on the south side." (p. 68)

65. Friday, December 29, 1620/January 8, 1621; Saturday, December 30, 1620/January 9, 1621.

66. Dexter reasons that the smoke was "in the direction of Duxbury, on the north, or of Telegraph Hill, on the south," since they could not see that distance inland and concludes that since "the Indians finally approached from the south, it is more probably that they were now lurking in that direction." (pp. 68-69)

67. Pointing out that Prince in his *Chronology* (p. 169) had indicated that Bradford ends his first book at this place, Young writes, "quite accurately, I conceive that much of this *Relation* is in substance, and often in language, Gov. Bradford's history." (p. 170)

68. Young conjectures that the *Mayflower* "probably anchored in the Cow Yard, an anchorage near Clarke's Island, which takes its name from a cow whale which once came into it, and was there killed." (p. 171) Dexter reasons that "If the harbor were then at all as now, (1865) or as it has been for the last hundred years, she probably lay at anchor in the channel just inside the end of the beach." (p. 69)

69. "The year begins with the death of Degory Priest." (Prince, p. 69)

70. January 13, 1621. (New style)

MOURT'S
RELATION:
A JOURNAL
OF THE
PILGRIMS OF
PLYMOUTH

A RELATION OR
JOURNAL OF THE
PROCEEDINGS OF
THE PLANTATION
SETTLED AT
PLYMOUTH IN
NEW ENGLAND

gather thatch, they saw great fires of the Indians, and were at their corn-fields, yet saw none of the savages, nor had seen any of them since we came to this bay.

Thursday, the fourth of January,[71] Captain Miles Standish with four or five more, went to see if they could meet with any of the savages in that place where the fires were made. They went to some of their houses, but not lately inhabited; yet could they not meet with any. As they came home, they shot at an eagle and killed her, which was excellent meat; it was hardly to be discerned from mutton.[72]

Friday, the 5th of January,[73] one of the sailors found alive upon the shore a herring, which the master had to his supper; which put us in hope of fish, but as yet we had got but one cod; we wanted small hooks.[74]

Saturday, the 6th of January,[75] Master Martin[76] was very sick, and, to our judgment, no hope of life. So Master Carver was sent for to come aboard to speak with him about his accounts; who came the next morning.

Monday, the eighth day of January,[77] was a very fair day, and we went betimes to work. Master Jones sent the shallop, as he had formerly done, to see where fish could be got. They had a great storm at sea, and were in some danger. At night they returned with three great seals,[78] and an excellent good cod, which did assure us that we should have plenty of fish shortly.

This day Francis Billington, having the week before seen from the top of a tree on a high hill a great sea,[79] as he thought, went with one of the master's mates to see it. They went three miles and then came to a great water, divided into two great lakes; the bigger of them five or six miles in circuit, and in it an isle of a cable length square; the other three miles in compass,[80] in their estimation. They are fine fresh water, full of fish and fowl. A brook[81] issues from it; it will be an excellent place for us in time.[82] They found seven or eight Indian houses, but not lately inhabited. When they saw the houses, they were in some fear; for they were but two persons and one piece.[83]

---

71. January 14, 1621. (n.s.)

72. They had undoubtedly had no mutton since leaving England.

73. January 15, 1621. (n.s.)

74. From this vantage point, it seems incredible that they could have forgotten such a valuable item. In his *Good News from New England* Winslow notes that they also needed "fit and strong seines and other netting." Dexter writes, "To this single circumstance much of their discomfort in regard to food was due." (p. 70)

75. January 16, 1621. (n.s.)

76. Christopher Martin had joined the company in England. According to Bradford, Martin had been selected with Carver and Cushman "to make the provisions for the voyage." He was chosen to represent the new English members of the company "not so much for any great needs of their help, as to avoid all supposition or jealousy of any partiality." This explains his need to settle accounts. He died two days later, January 8/18, 1621.

77. January 18, 1621. (n.s.)

78. Seals are still seen occasionally off Cape Cod.

79. Billington Sea, which is really a pond. For a century after its discovery it was known as Fresh Lake.

80. The description of Billington Sea is accurate, except for the distance, which is about two miles. Young waxed poetic over the pond 135 years ago: "It is now, as at first, embosomed in a wilderness of woods. The eagle still sails over it, and builds in the branches of the surrounding forest. Here the loon cries, and leaves her eggs on the shore of the smaller island. Here too the beautiful wood-duck finds a sequestered retreat; and the fallow deer, mindful of their ancient haunts still resort to it to drink and to browse on its margin." (p. 172)

81. Town Brook, which passes through Plymouth and empties into the harbor south of Plymouth Rock. Young writes, "Before the brook was so much impeded by dams, vast quantities of alewives passed up it annually to Billington Sea." (p. 172)

82. Bradford had no idea how prophetic he was. For many years Town Brook supplied the water power for most of Plymouth's early manufacturing plants.

83. They undoubtedly belonged to Indians who had died in the plague a few years earlier.

Tuesday, the 9th of January,[84] was a reasonable fair day; and we went to labor that day in the building of our town, in two rows of houses, for more safety.[85] We divided by lot the plot of ground whereon to build our town, after the proportion formerly allotted.[86] We agreed that every man should build his own house, thinking by that course men would make more haste than working in common.[87] The common house,[88] in which for the first we made our rendezvous,[89] being near finished, wanted only covering, it being about twenty foot square. Some should make mortar, and some gather thatch; so that in four days half of it was thatched. Frost and foul weather hindered us much.[90] This time of the year seldom could we work half the week.[91]

Thursday, the eleventh, William Bradford[92] being at work, (for it was a fair day,) was vehemently taken with a grief and pain, and so shot to his huckle-bone,[93] it was doubted that he would have instantly died. He got cold in the former discoveries, especially the last; and felt some pain in his ankles by times; but he grew a little better towards night, and in time, through God's mercy in the use of means, recovered.

Friday the 12th[94] we went to work; but about noon it began to rain, that it forced us to give over work.

This day two of our people put us in great sorrow and care. There was four sent to gather and cut thatch in the morning; and two of them John Goodman[95] and Peter Browne,[96] having cut thatch[97] all the forenoon, went to a further place, and willed the other two to bind up that which was cut, and to follow them. So they did, being about a mile and a half from our plantation. But when the two came after, they could not find them, nor hear any thing of them at all, though they hallooed and shouted as loud as they could. So they returned to the company, and told them of it. Whereupon Master Carver[98] and three or four more went to seek them; but could hear nothing of them. So they returning, sent more; but that night they could hear nothing at all of them. The next day they armed ten or twelve men out, verily thinking the Indians had surprised them. They went seeking seven or eight miles; but could neither see nor hear any thing at all. So they returned, with much discomfort to us all.

---

84. January 19, 1621. (n.s.)

85. Young notes, "The houses were built on each side of Leyden Street, which extends from the First Church to the harbor." (p. 173)

86. See notes 62-64. (p. 39)

87. Obviously this was excellent psychology.

88. Dexter writes, "This stood . . . on the south side of Leyden Street, near the declivity of the hill toward the water side." (p. 72)

89. Freeman notes that "On the spot where it is supposed the common house stood, in 1801, there were discovered sundry tools and a plate of iron, seven feet below the surface of the ground." (p. 173)

90. "Although they had many rainy days, the winter was doubtless more favorable than the average to their work." (Dexter, p. 72)

91. Most persons engaged in outdoor construction in southeastern Massachusetts would probably be satisfied if they could "work half the week," in January.

92. January 21, 1621. (n.s.) The failure to include *Mr.* before his name indicates that Bradford was as Dexter indicates "the modest penman of this part of this narrative." (p. 72)

93. Hip-bone.

94. January 22, 1621. (n.s.)

95. John Goodman was granted the first lot east of Elder Brewster's, but he died that first winter.

96. Peter Browne later settled in Duxbury where he died in October, 1633.

97. The coarse grass and reeds that could be used to roof their houses as they did in England.

98. In the original printing it appears as *Seaver,* an obvious misprint.

MOURT'S
RELATION:
A JOURNAL
OF THE
PILGRIMS OF
PLYMOUTH

A RELATION OR
JOURNAL OF THE
PROCEEDINGS OF
THE PLANTATION
SETTLED AT
PLYMOUTH IN
NEW ENGLAND

These two that were missed at dinner time, took their meat in their hands, and would go walk and refresh themselves. So going a little off, they find a lake of water,[99] and having a great mastiff bitch[100] with them and a spaniel, by the water side they found a great deer.[101] The dogs chased him; and they followed so far as they lost themselves, and they could not find the way back. They wandered all that afternoon, being wet; and at night it did freeze and snow. They were slenderly apparelled, and had no weapons but each one his sickle, nor any victuals. They ranged up and down and could find none of the savages' habitations. When it drew to night, they were much perplexed; for they could find neither harbor nor meat; but, in frost and snow, were forced to make the earth their bed and the element their covering. And another thing did very much terrify them; they heard, as they thought, two lions[102] roaring exceedingly for a long time together, and a third that they thought was very near them. So not knowing what to do, they resolved to climb up into a tree, as their safest refuge, though that would prove an intolerable cold lodging. So they stood at the tree's root, that when the lions came, they might take their opportunity of climbing up. The bitch they were fain to hold by the neck, for she would have been gone to the lion. But it pleased God so to dispose, that the wild beasts came not. So they walked up and down under the tree all night. It was an extreme cold night. So soon as it was light,[103] they travelled again, passing by many lakes[104] and brooks and woods, and in one place where the savages had burnt the space of five miles in length, which is a fine champaign country, and even.[105] In the afternoon, it pleased God from a high hill they discovered the two[106] isles in the bay, and so that night got to the plantation, being ready to faint with travail and want of victuals, and almost famished with cold. John Goodman was fain to have his shoes cut off his feet, they were so swelled with cold; and it was a long while after ere he was able to go. Those on the shore were much comforted at their return, but they on shipboard were grieved at deeming them lost.

But the next day, being the 14th of January,[107] in the morning about six of the clock, the wind being very great, they on shipboard spied their great new rendezvous on fire; which was to them a new discomfort, fearing, because of the supposed loss of the men, that the savages had fired them. Neither could they presently go to them for want of water. But after three quarters of an hour they went, as they had

---

99. Young believes this to be "Murdock's Pond, about half a mile from the village in the rear of Burial hill. It is a deep, round pond." (p. 175) Dexter believes this to be "Lout Pond, which is a small lake perhaps a quarter of a mile in length, a little E. of Billington Sea." (p. 74) Having walked over much of the area, this editor leans to Dexter's thesis.

100. The mastiff has always been an excellent hunting and watch dog. Gosnold and Brereton brought mastiffs with them to Massachusetts eighteen years earlier.

101. There are still plenty of deer in the area.

102. Many writers who dealt with seventeenth century New England referred to the "lions" there. Freeman observes that Goodman and Brown, coming from England where both the lion and wolf were unknown, mistook the howling of wolves for the roaring of lions.

103. Saturday, January 13/23, 1621.

104. It is estimated that there are about 200 ponds in the town of Plymouth. The Pilgrims evidently used the terms *ponds* and *lakes* interchangeably.

105. Freeman notes that "A plain commences two miles from the town, and extends six miles southwest." Dexter says that this account "very accurately describes the characteristics of the country for several miles around Great South Pond as a center, four or five miles s. of Plymouth Rock." (p. 76)

106. See note 4. (p. 35)

107. Sunday, January 14/24, 1621.

MOURT'S
RELATION:
A JOURNAL
OF THE
PILGRIMS OF
PLYMOUTH

A RELATION OR
JOURNAL OF THE
PROCEEDINGS OF
THE PLANTATION
SETTLED AT
PLYMOUTH IN
NEW ENGLAND

purposed the day before to keep the Sabbath on shore, because now there was the greater number of people.[108] At their landing they heard good tidings of the return of the two men, and that the house was fired occasionally[109] by a spark that flew into the thatch, which instantly burnt it all up; but the roof stood, and little hurt.[110] The most loss was Master Carver's and William Bradford's,[111] who then lay sick in bed, and if they had not risen with good speed, had been blown up with powder; but, through God's mercy, they had no harm. The house was as full of beds as they could lie one by another, and their muskets charged; but, blessed be God, there was no harm done.

Monday, the 15th day,[112] it rained much all day, that they on shipboard could not go on shore, nor they on shore do any labor, but were all wet.

Tuesday, Wednesday, Thursday, were very fair, sunshiny days, as if it had been in April; and our people, so many as were in health, wrought cheerfully.

The 19th day,[113] we resolved to make a shed to put our common provision in, of which some were already set on shore; but at noon it rained, that we could not work. This day, in the evening, John Goddman went abroad to use his lame feet, that were pitifully ill with the cold he had got, having a little spaniel with him. A little way from the plantation two great wolves ran after the dog; the dog ran to him and betwixt his legs for succour. He had nothing in his hand, but took up a stick and threw at one of them and hit him, and they presently ran both away, but came again. He got a pale-board[114] in his hand; and they sat both on their tails grinning at him a good while; and went their way and left him.

Saturday, 20th, we made up our shed for our common goods.

Sunday, the 21st, we kept our meeting on land.[115]

Monday, the 22nd, was a fair day.[116] We wrought on our houses; and in the afternoon carried up our hogsheads of meal to our common storehouse. The rest of the week we followed our business likewise.

Monday, the 29th,[117] in the morning, cold, frost, and sleet; but after reasonable fair. Both the long-boat and the shallop brought our common goods on shore.

Tuesday and Wednesday, 30th and 31st of January,[118] cold, frosty weather and sleet, that we could not work. In the morning, the master and others saw two savages, that had been on the island near our ship. What they came for we could not tell. They were going[119] so far back again before they were descried, that we could not speak with them.

Sunday, the 4th of February,[120] was very wet and rainy, with the greatest gusts of

---

108. This was probably the first Sunday that they spent ashore. Since there had been a fire, it must be supposed that their first Sabbath service must have been held the following week.

109. Occasionally = casually, accidentally.

110. Evidently the thatched roof was destroyed but the framework of the roof and the rafters were intact.

111. Again Bradford's modesty shows through. Note he writes *Master* Carver but simply William Bradford.

112. January, 25, 1621. (n.s.)

113. Friday, January 29, 1621. (n.s.)

114. Pale-board—a stake.

115. Sunday, January 21/31, 1621, was the day of the first Sabbath in the meeting house. Undoubtedly, Elder William Brewster, who was one of the few spared from illness that winter, conducted the service.

116. Monday, February 1, 1621. (n.s.)

117. Monday, January 29/February 8, 1621. Rose Standish, wife of Myles Standish, died on this day.

118. January 30-31/February 9-10, 1621.

119. Young believes (p. 179) that this is a typographical error for *gone*.

120. February 14, 1621. (new style)

MOURT'S
RELATION:
A JOURNAL
OF THE
PILGRIMS OF
PLYMOUTH

A RELATION OR
JOURNAL OF THE
PROCEEDINGS OF
THE PLANTATION
SETTLED AT
PLYMOUTH IN
NEW ENGLAND

wind that ever we had since we came forth; that though we rid in a very good harbor, yet we were in danger, because our ship was light, the goods taken out, and she unballasted; and it caused much daubing of our houses to fall down.[121]

Friday, the 9th,[122] still the cold weather continued, that we could do little work. That afternoon, our little house for our sick people[123] was set on fire by a spark that kindled in the roof; but no great harm was done. That evening, the master[124] going ashore, killed five geese, which he friendly distributed among the sick people. He found also a good deer killed. The savages had cut off the horns, and a wolf was eating of him. How he came there we could not conceive.

Friday, the 16th,[125] was a fair day; but the northerly wind continued, which continued the frost. This day, after noon, one of our people being a fowling, and having taken a stand by a creek side in the reeds, about a mile and a half from our plantation, there by him twelve Indians, marching towards our plantation, and in the woods he heard the noise of many more. He lay close till they were passed, and then with what speed he could he went home and gave the alarm. So the people abroad in the woods returned and armed themselves, but saw none of them; only, toward the evening, they made a great fire about the place where they were first discovered. Captain Miles Standish and Francis Cooke[126] being at work in the woods, coming home left their tools behind them; but before they returned, their tools were taken away by the savages. This coming of the savages gave us occasion to keep more strict watch, and to make our pieces and furniture ready, which by the moisture and rain were out of temper.

Saturday, the 17th day,[127] in the morning, we called a meeting for the establishing of military orders among ourselves; and we chose Miles Standish our captain, and gave him authority of command in affairs. And as we were in consultation hereabouts, two savages presented themselves upon the top of a hill,[128] over against our plantation, about a quarter of a mile and less, and made signs unto us to come unto them; we likewise made signs unto them to come to us. Whereupon we armed ourselves and stood ready, and sent two over the brook,[129] towards them, to wit, Captain Standish and Stephen Hopkins,[130] who went towards them. Only one of them had a musket, which they laid down on the ground in their sight, in sign of peace and to parley with them. But the savages would not tarry their coming. A noise of a great many more was heard behind the hill; but no more came in sight.

---

121. Young (p. 179) erroneously believes that the Pilgrims built "log-huts" as does Dexter (p. 79). The space between the planks was filled with clay mortar, and the driving storm evidently dislodged some.

122. January 19, 1621. (n.s.)

123. Obviously the common house, now completed, was needed at once for a hospital.

124. The reference is to Captain Jones.

125. January 26, 1621. (n.s.)

126. Francis Cooke came over on the *Mayflower* with his John and both survived that first winter. His wife, Esther, and three children arrived on the *Anne* in 1623, and their daughter Mary was born in 1626. His name appears often in the public records. Bradford writes in 1650 that he has lived to be "a very old man, and hath seen his children's children have children." Francis Cooke was a purchaser of Dartmouth in 1652 and of Middleboro in 1662. He died on April 17, 1663. (n.s.)

127. January 27, 1621. (n.s.)

128. Watson's Hill or Strawberry Hill about 3/10 of a mile south west of the village. Young writes (p. 180) that the "Indian name was Cantaugcanteest." When the summit of the hill was leveled in 1814, Indian relics of various kinds were found.

129. Town Brook.

130. See note 54. (p. 16)

MOURT'S
RELATION:
A JOURNAL
OF THE
PILGRIMS OF
PLYMOUTH

A RELATION OR
JOURNAL OF THE
PROCEEDINGS OF
THE PLANTATION
SETTLED AT
PLYMOUTH IN
NEW ENGLAND

This caused us to plant our great ordnances in places most convenient.

Wednesday, the 21st of February,[131] the master came on shore, with many of his sailors, and brought with him one of the great pieces, called a minion,[132] and helped us to draw it up the hill, with another piece that lay on shore, and mounted them, and a saker[133] and two bases.[134] He brought with him a very fat goose to eat with us, and we had a fat crane and a mallard, and a dried neat's tongue;[135] and so we were kindly and friendly together.[136]

Saturday, the third of March, the wind was south, the morning misty, but towards noon warm and fair weather. The birds sang in the woods most pleasantly. At one of the clock it thundered, which was the first we heard in that country. It was strong and great claps, but short; but after an hour it rained very sadly till midnight.

Wednesday, the seventh of March, the wind was full east, cold, but fair. That day Master Carver with five others went to the great ponds,[137] which seem to be excellent fishing places. All the way they went they found it exceedingly beaten, and haunted with deer; but they saw none. Amongst other fowl they saw one, a milk-white fowl, with a very black head. This day some garden seeds were sown.

Friday, the 16th, a fair warm day towards.[138] This morning we determined to conclude of the military orders, which we had begun to consider of before, but were interrupted by the savages, as we mentioned formerly. And whilst we were busied hereabout, we were interrupted again; for there presented himself a savage,[139] which caused an alarm. He very boldly came all alone, and along the house, straight to the rendezvous; where we intercepted him, not suffering him to go in,[140] as undoubtedly he would out of his boldness. He saluted us in English, and bade us "Welcome!" for he had learned some broken English among the Englishmen that came to fish at Monhegan[141] and knew by name the most of the captains, commanders, and masters, that usually come. He was a man free in speech, so far as he could express his mind, and of a seemly carriage. We questioned him of many things; he was the first savage we could meet withal. He said he was not of these parts, but of Morattig-gon,[142] and one of the sagamores or lords thereof; and had been eight months in these parts, it lying hence a day's sail with a great wind, and five days by land. He

---

131. Wednesday, February 21/March 13, 1621.

132. Dexter notes, "There were two sizes of *minions* — one of 3½-inch bore and 8 feet in length, carrying a ball weighing 3 lbs. 12 oz.; the smaller, of 3-inch bore, and 7 feet long. The first weighed about 1,000 lbs., and the second about 800 lbs." (p. 81)

133. In the original the word is *saller,* a misprint.

134. Dexter defines the *base* as "the smallest piece of ordnance, 4½ feet long, the diameter at the bore 1¼ inches; it weighs 200 pounds, carries a ball 1⅛ inches in diameter and five or six ounces weight." (p. 82)

135. *Neat* is an archaic word meaning a domestic bovine.

136. William White and William Mullens die on this day.

137. "Billington Sea, or, possibly, Great South Pond and its sisterhood of lakes." (Dexter, p. 82)

138. The word *noon* was probably omitted here. March 26, 1621.

139. This was Samoset (whose name appears on the records as *Samaset, Summuset, Sommerset,* and *Sommersant*), a native of Pemaquid in Maine. In the spring before the arrival of the Pilgrims he was landed by Captain Dermer on Cape Cod and he redeemed several shipwrecked Frenchmen from their Indian captivity. He lived in Maine for 30 or 40 years after the Pilgrims arrived.

140. "They were unwilling he should see how few and weak they were." (Young, p. 182)

141. Monhegan Island (spelled *Monhiggon* in the original) off the coast of Maine "lies nine miles southerly of George's Islands, five leagues east south-easterly of Townsend, and three leagues westwardly of Metinic, . . . It contains more than one thousand acres of good land, with a bold shore." (Dexter, pp. 83-84)

142. Probably an error for *Monhegan.*

MOURT'S
RELATION:
A JOURNAL
OF THE
PILGRIMS OF
PLYMOUTH

A RELATION OR
JOURNAL OF THE
PROCEEDINGS OF
THE PLANTATION
SETTLED AT
PLYMOUTH IN
NEW ENGLAND

discoursed[143] of the whole country, and of every province, and of their sagamores, and their number of men and strength. The wind beginning to rise a little, we cast a horseman's coat about him; for he was stark naked, only a leather about his waist, with a fringe about a span long or little more. He had a bow and two arrows, the one headed, and the other unheaded. He was a tall, straight man, the hair of his head black, long behind, only short before, none on his face at all. He asked some beer, but we gave him strong water, and biscuit, and butter, and cheese, and pudding, and a piece of mallard; all which he liked well, and had been acquainted with such amongst the English. He told us the place where we now live is called Patuxet,[144] and that about four years ago all the inhabitants died of an extraordinary plague,[145] and there is neither man, woman, nor child remaining, as indeed we have found none; so as there is none to hinder our possession, or to lay claim unto it. All the afternoon we spent in communication with him. We would gladly have been rid of him at night, but he was not willing to go this night. Then we thought to carry him on shipboard, wherewith he was well content, and went into the shallop; but the wind was high and the water scant, that it could not return back. We lodged him that night at Stephen Hopkin's house,[146] and watched him.

The next day he went away back to the Massasoits[147] from whence he said he came, who are our next bordering neighbors. They are sixty strong, as he saith. The Nausets are as near, southeast of them, and are a hundred strong; and those were they of whom our people were encountered, as we before related. They are much incensed and provoked against the English; and about eight months ago slew three Englishmen, and two more hardly escaped by flight to Monhegan. They were Sir Ferdinando Gorge's[148] men, as this savage told us; as he did likewise of the *huggery*, that is, fight,[149] that our discoverers had with the Nausets, and of our tools that were taken out of the woods, which we willed him should be brought again; otherwise we could right ourselves. These people are ill affected towards the English by reason of one Hunt,[150] a master of a ship, who deceived the people and got them,

---

143. One wonders at the extent of Samoset's vocabulary. Samoset probably thought the *Mayflower* was just another fishing vessel and "this explains his boldness in coming directly to them." (Young, pp. 182-183)

144. John Smith indicated that the Indian name for Plymouth was Accomack. Dexter (p. 85) believes that *Patuxet* was probably the name given to it by the Massachusetts and other northern tribes."

145. Young notes, "All the early writers on New England agree, that for three or four years previous to the arrival of the Pilgrims, a deadly pestilence had raged all along the seaboard, from the *Penobscot* to Narragansett Bay. The two tribes dwelling at these extremes, as well as the *Nauset* Indians, on Cape Cod, escaped, whilst the intermediate inhabitants were almost entirely swept off." (pp. 183-184)

146. According to Dexter, "This makes it probable that they had already completed some of their cottages, and that families had moved into them." (p. 85)

147. Massasoit was the leader of the Pokonoket Indians who lived in Sowams in present day Bristol Neck, R.I.

148. Young refers to *Gorges' Brief Narration,* in which the author mentions an attack that was made in July, 1620, by the Indians of Martha's Vineyard on Capt. Dermer and his company, whom he had sent over to New England. Dermer lost all his men but one, and received fourteen wounds in this encounter; which took place just eight months before; and these were the 'Sir Ferdinando Gorges' men' mentioned in the text. Dermer had previously been at Nautreat, or Nauset." (pp. 185-186)

149. Hugger = to lie in ambush.

150. Thomas Hunt, master of a ship in John Smith's company in 1614. His name "has come down to us loaded with deserved infamy, as the first kidnapper and slave-dealer on the coast of North America. There is a difference in the accounts of the number of the natives which he thus seized and carried off. The President and Council of New England, in their *Brief Relation of its Discovery and Plantations,* stated the number as 24; Gorges mentions 30; whilst Capt. John Smith, says 27, agreeing with the number mentioned in the text. Hunt carried the Indians to Spain, where they were humanely rescued and set at liberty by the monks of *Malaga.* Several of them got over to England, and proved of essential service to Gorges." (Young, p. 186)

MOURT'S
RELATION:
A JOURNAL
OF THE
PILGRIMS OF
PLYMOUTH

A RELATION OR
JOURNAL OF THE
PROCEEDINGS OF
THE PLANTATION
SETTLED AT
PLYMOUTH IN
NEW ENGLAND

under color of trucking with them, twenty out of this very place were we inhabit, and seven men from the Nausets[151] and carried them away, and sold them for slaves, like a wretched man (for twenty pound a man,) that cares not what mischief he doth for his profit.

Saturday, in the morning,[152] we dismissed the savage, and gave him a knife, a bracelet, and a ring. He promised within a night or two to come again and to bring with him some of the Massasoits, our neighbors, with such beavers' skins as they had to truck with us.

Saturday and Sunday[153] reasonable fair days. On this day[154] came again the savage, and brought with him five other tall, proper men. They had every man a deer's skin on him, and the principal of them had a wild cat's skin, or such like, on the one arm. They had most of them long hosen[155] up to their groins, close made, and above their groins to their waist another leather; they were altogether like the Irish trousers.[156] They are of complexion like our English gypsies; no hair or very little on their faces; on their heads long hair to their shoulders, only cut before; some trussed up before with a feather, broad-wise, like a fan; another a fox tail, hanging out. These left (according to our charge given him before) their bows and arrows a quarter of a mile from our town. We gave them entertainment as we thought was fitting them. They did eat liberally of our English victuals. They made semblance unto us of friendship and amity. They sang and danced after their manner, like antics. They brought with them in a thing like a bow-case, (which the principal of them had about his waist,) a little of their corn pounded to powder, which, put to a little water, they eat.[157] He had a little tobacco in a bag; but none of them drank[158] but when he liked. Some of them had their faces painted black, from the forehead to the chin, four or five fingers broad; others after other fashions, as they liked. They brought three or four skins; but we would not truck with them at all that day,[159] but wished them to bring more, and we would truck for all; which they promised within a night or two, and would leave these behind them, though we were not willing they should; and they brought us all our tools again, which were taken in the woods, in our men's absence. So, because of the day, we dismissed them so soon as we could. But Samoset, our first acquaintance, either was sick or feigned himself so, and would not go with them, and stayed with us till Wednesday morning.[160] Then we sent him to them, to know the reason they come not according to their words; and we gave

---

151. The same Indians the Pilgrims had met in the First Encounter.

152. Saturday, March 17/27, 1621.

153. Sunday, March 18/28, 1621.

154. Sunday.

155. Leggings.

156. Thomas Morton in *New English Canaan* writes, "They make shoes of deer's skins, very handsomely and commodious, and of such deer's skins as they dress bare, they make stockings, that come within their shoes, like a stirrup stocking, and is fastened above at their belt, which is about their middle. . . . Those garments they always put on when they go ahunting to keep their skins from the brush of the shrubs, and when they have their apparel on, they look like Irish in their trousers, the stocking just so to their breeches." W. Wood in his *New England's Prospect* (Part II, Ch. 5) writes that "in the winter time the more aged of them wear leather drawers, in form like Irish trousers, fastened under their girdles with buttons."

157. This is *nokehick* or *nokake* meal made of parched corn and water. Several seventeenth century writers mention this staple dish.

158. The use of the word *drinking* for *smoking* tobacco was common in this period.

159. The Sabbath day.

160. Wednesday, March 21/31, 1621.

MOURT'S
RELATION:
A JOURNAL
OF THE
PILGRIMS OF
PLYMOUTH

A RELATION OR
JOURNAL OF THE
PROCEEDINGS OF
THE PLANTATION
SETTLED AT
PLYMOUTH IN
NEW ENGLAND

him a hat, a pair of stockings and shoes, a shirt, and a piece of cloth to tie about his waist.

The Sabbath day, when we sent them from us, we gave every one of them some trifles, especially the principal of them. We carried them, along with our arms, to the place where they left their bows and arrows; whereat they were amazed, and two of them began to slink away, but that the other called them. When they took their arrows we bade them farewell, and they were glad; and so, with many thanks given us, they departed, with promise they would come again.

Monday and Tuesday proved fair days. We digged our grounds and sowed our garden seeds.

Wednesday a fine warm day. We sent away Samoset.

That day we had again a meeting to conclude of laws and order for ourselves, and to confirm those military orders that were formerly propounded, and twice broken off by the savages coming. But so we were again the third time; for after we had been an hour together, on the top of the hill[161] over against us two or three savages presented themselves, that made semblance of daring us, as we thought. So Captain Standish with another, with their muskets, went over to them, with two of the master's mates that follows them without arms,[162] having two muskets with them. They whetted and rubbed their arrows and strings, and made show of defiance; but when our men drew near them, they ran away. Thus were we again interrupted by them. This day, with much ado, we got our carpenter, that had been long sick of the scurvy, to fit our shallop to fetch all from aboard.[163]

Thursday, the 22nd of March, was a very fair, warm day. About noon we met again about our public business. But we had scarce been an hour together, but Samoset came again, and Squanto,[164] the only native of Patuxet, where we now inhabit, who was one of the twenty captives that by Hunt were carried away, and had been in England, and dwelt in Cornhill with Master John Slany[165] a merchant, and could speak a little English, with three others; and they brought with them some few skins to truck, and some red herrings, newly taken and dried, but not salted; and signified unto us, that their great sagamore, Massasoit,[166] was hard by, with Quadequina, his brother, and all their men. They could not express well in English what

---

161. Watson's Hill or Strawberry Hill, the same hill on which the two Indians had appeared on February 17.

162. Side arms, swords, etc. They had their muskets.

163. Dexter writes that "This indicates the time when the whole company was transferred from the ship to the shore, and their colonizing became complete." (p. 90)

164. Squanto, *Squantum, Tisquantum,* according to Dexter, "was clearly one of five Indians who had been carried to England by Capt. George Waymouth, in 1605." (p. 90) Dexter conjectures that he had been returned and probably was taken off again by Hunt in 1614. It is certain that Dermer used Squanto's services earlier in 1620 and that probably in June, when Dermer left for Virginia, he left the Indian near Saco in Maine, and Squanto returned to Patuxet and Nemasket. (Young, pp. 190-191) Dexter credits him with being "of great service to the colony, though ambitious and meddlesome. He died in November, 1622; his last request being that Gov. Bradford would pray that he might go to the Englishman's God in heaven." (pp. 90-91)

165. He was a London merchant who was Treasurer of the Newfoundland Company.

166. Massasoit (Messasoyt, Massasoyet, Woomsamequin, Ussamiquin, Ashumiquin, Osamekem, Ousemaquin) "was sachem of the Wampanoags, and had his principal residence at Sowams (now Warren, R.I.), in Qokonoket. In 1623 he was very sick; and Winslow visited him and prescribed for him, and he recovered, and attributed his life to this attention. He sold much land to the English at various times, and always scrupulously, and most honorably, kept his treaty engagements with them. He seems to have died in the latter part of 1661, or the former part of 1662." (Dexter, p. 91)

MOURT'S
RELATION:
A JOURNAL
OF THE
PILGRIMS OF
PLYMOUTH

A RELATION OR
JOURNAL OF THE
PROCEEDINGS OF
THE PLANTATION
SETTLED AT
PLYMOUTH IN
NEW ENGLAND

they would;[167] but after an hour the king came to the top of a hill[168] over against us, and had in his train sixty men, that we could well behold them, and they us. We were not willing to send our governor to them, and they were[169] unwilling to come to us. So Squanto went again unto him, who brought word that we should send one to parley with him, which we did, which was Edward Winsloe, to know his mind, and signify the mind and will of our Governor, which was to have trading and peace with him. We sent to the king a pair of knives, and a copper chain with a jewel at it. To Quadequina we sent likewise a knife, and a jewel to hang in his ear, and withal a pot of strong water, a good quantity of biscuit, and some butter; which were all willingly accepted.

Our messenger made a speech unto him, that King James saluted him with words of love and peace, and did accept of him as his friend and ally; and that our governor desired to see him and to truck with him, and to confirm a peace with him, as his next neighbor. He liked well of the speech, and heard it attentively, though the interpreters did not well express it. After he had eaten and drunk himself, and given the rest to his company, he looked upon our messenger's sword and armor, which he had on, with intimation of his desire to buy it; but, on the other side, our messenger showed his unwillingness to part with it. In the end, he left him in the custody of Quadequina, his brother, and came over the brook, and some twenty men following him, leaving all their bows and arrows behind them. We kept six or seven as hostages for our messenger. Captain Standish and Master Williamson[170] met the king at the brook, with half a dozen musketeers. They saluted him, and he them; so one going over, the one on the one side, and the other on the other, conducted him to a house then in building, where we placed a green rug and three or four cushions. Then instantly came our governor, with drum and trumpet after him, and some few musketeers. After salutations, our governor kissing his hand, the king kissed him; and so they sat down. The governor called for some strong water, and drunk to him; and he drunk a great draught, that made his sweat all the while after. He called for a little fresh meat, which the king did eat willingly, and did give his followers. Then they treated of peace, which was:

1. That neither he nor any of his should injure or do hurt to any of our people.

2. And if any of his did hurt to any of ours, he should send the offender, that we might punish him.

3. That if any of our tools were taken away, when our people were at work, he should cause them to be restored; and if ours did any harm to any of his, we would do the like to them.

4. If any did unjustly war against him, we would aid him; if any did war against us, he should aid us.

5. He should send to his neighbor confederates to certify them of this, that they might not wrong us, but might be likewise comprised in the conditions of peace.

167. See note 147. (p. 46)
168. Watson's Hill.
169. The word *were* is omitted in the original.
170. There was no "Master Williamson" in the company. There was a Thomas Williams who died early that winter. Young thinks (p. 192) that "perhaps it should read Master Allerton," which is a reasonable conjecture. Some students believe that this is an *alias* for William Brewster, whose name appears to be carefully omitted from this account.

MOURT'S
RELATION:
A JOURNAL
OF THE
PILGRIMS OF
PLYMOUTH

A RELATION OR
JOURNAL OF THE
PROCEEDINGS OF
THE PLANTATION
SETTLED AT
PLYMOUTH IN
NEW ENGLAND

6. That when their men came to us, they should leave their bows and arrows behind them, as we should do our pieces when we came to them.

Lastly, that doing thus, King James would esteem of him as his friend and ally.[171]

All of which the king seemed to like well, and it was applauded of his followers. All the while he sat by the governor, he trembled for fear. In his person he is a very lusty man, in his best years, an able body, grave of countenance, and spare of speech; in his attire little or nothing differing from the rest of his followers, only in a great chain of white bone beads about his neck; and at it, behind his neck, hangs a little bag of tobacco, which he drank,[172] and gave us to drink. His face was painted with a sad red, like murrey,[173] and oiled both head and face, that he looked greasily. All his followers likewise were in their faces, in part or in whole, painted, some black, some red, some yellow, and some white, some with crosses, and other antic works;[174] some had skins on them, and some naked; all strong, tall men in appearance.

So after all was done, the governor conducted him to the brook, and there they embraced each other, and he departed; we diligently keeping our hostages. We expected our messenger's coming; but anon word was brought us that Quadequina was coming, and our messenger was stayed till his return; who presently came, and a troop with him. So likewise we entertained him, and conveyed him to the place prepared. He was very fearful of our pieces, and made signs of dislike, that they should be carried away; whereupon commandment was given they should be laid away. He was a very proper, tall young man, of a very modest and seemly countenance, and he did kindly like of our entertainment. So we conveyed him likewise, as we did the king; but divers of their people stayed still. When he was returned, then they dismissed our messenger. Two of his people would have stayed all night; but we would not suffer it. One thing I forgot; the king had in his bosom, hanging in a string, a great long knife. He marvelled much at our trumpet, and some of his men would sound it as well as they could. Samoset and Squanto, they stayed all night with us; and the king and all his men lay all night in the woods, not above half an English mile from us, and all their wives and women with them. They said that within eight or nine days they would come and set corn on the other side of the brook, and dwell there all summer; which is hard by us. That night we kept good watch; but there was no appearance of danger.

The next morning, divers of their people came over to us, hoping to get some victuals, as we imagined. Some of them told us the king would have some of us come see him. Captain Standish and Isaac Allerton[175] went venturously, who were welcomed of him after their manner. He gave them three or four groundnuts and some tobacco. We cannot yet conceive but that he is willing to have peace with us; for they have seen our people sometimes alone two or three in the woods at work and

---

171. This treaty was kept by both sides for 55 years. On September 25/October 5, 1639, this was formally ratified and renewed by the Plymouth General Court at the request of Massasoit and his eldest son, Mooanam, later called Wamsutta or Alexander. (P.C.R., I, 133)

172. See note 158. (p. 47)

173. A dark red color from the Latin word for *mulberry*.

174. An *antic* was a clown or fool or buffoon.

175. Isaac Allerton of London was admitted to citizenship in Leyden February 7, 1615, and became a leader in the venture. He was assistant in 1621 and married as his second wife, Fear Brewster, William Brewster's daughter. He left Plymouth before March, 1647, and died in New Haven in 1659.

MOURT'S
RELATION:
A JOURNAL
OF THE
PILGRIMS OF
PLYMOUTH

A RELATION OR
JOURNAL OF THE
PROCEEDINGS OF
THE PLANTATION
SETTLED AT
PLYMOUTH IN
NEW ENGLAND

fowling, whenas they offered them no harm, as they might easily have done; and especially because he hath a potent adversary, the Narowhigansets, that are at war with him, against whom he thinks we may be some strength to him; for our pieces are terrible unto them. This morning they stayed till ten or eleven of the clock; and our governor bid them send the king's kettle, and filled it full of peas, which pleased them well; and so they went their way.

Friday[176] was a very fair day. Samoset and Squanto still remained with us. Squanto went at noon to fish for eels.[177] At night he came home with as many as he could well lift in one hand; which our people were glad of; they were fat and sweet. He trod them out[178] with his feet, and so caught them with his hands, without any other instrument.

This day we proceeded on with our common business, from which we had been so often hindered by the savages' coming and concluded both of military orders and of some laws[179] and orders as we thought behooveful for our present estate and condition; and did likewise choose[180] our governor for this year, which was Master John Carver, a man well approved amongst us.

---

176. Friday, March 23/April 2, 1621. The next day Elizabeth Winslow, wife of Edward Winslow, died.

177. Both Dexter (p. 97) and Young (p. 196) place the site of the fishing at Eel River "so called from the abundance of eels which are taken there." In the nineteenth century James Thacher, Plymouth's historian, indicated that they were still plentiful for "the support of the industrious poor," and he adds, "Perhaps it will not be extravagant to say that about 150 barrels are annually taken there." (*History of Plymouth,* p. 322).

178. Of the mud.

179. These were basic laws for the operation of the colony and were eventually incorporated in the code of laws passed in 1636.

180. Carver had been chosen before they left, again aboard the *Mayflower* in Provincetown harbor, and now at Plymouth. Carver died in April, and his wife died in May.

"The Signing of the *Mayflower Compact*, 1620"
Courtesy of the Pilgrim Society

A Journey to Packanokik, the Habitation of the Great King Massasoit: As also Our Message, the Answer and Entertainment We Had of Him[1]

It seemed good to the company, for many considerations, to send some amongst them to Massasoit, the greatest commander amongst the savages bordering upon us; partly to know where to find them, if occasion served, as also to see their strength, discover the country, prevent abuses in their disorderly coming unto us, make satisfaction for some conceived injuries to be done on our parts, and to continue the league of peace and friendship between them and us. For these and the like ends it pleased the governor to make choice of Stephen Hopkins and Edward Winslow to go unto him; and having a fit opportunity, by reason of a savage called Tisquantum, that could speak English, coming unto us, with all expedition provided a horseman's coat of red cotton, and laced with a slight lace, for a present, that both they and their message might be the more acceptable amongst them.

The message was as follows: That forasmuch as his subjects came often and without fear upon all occasions amongst us, so we were now come unto him; and in witness of the love and good-will the English bear unto him, the governor hath sent him a coat, desiring that the peace and amity that was between them and us might be continued; not that we feared them, but because we intended not to injure any, desiring to live peaceably, and as with all men, so especially with them, our nearest neighbors. But whereas his people came very often, and very many together unto us, bringing for the most part their wives and children with them, they were welcome; yet we being but strangers as yet at Patuxet, alias New Plymouth,[2] and

---

1. This narrative is obviously the work of Edward Winslow, who went on the expedition. There is much internal evidence in spelling of certain words and proper names and in the language used to ascribe it to Winslow.

2. Captain John Smith designates the place as Plymouth in his map of New England published in 1616. N. Morton in his *New England's Memorial* writes, "The name of Plymouth was so called . . . because Plymouth in Old England, was the last town they left in their native country; and for that they had received many kindnesses there."

MOURT'S
RELATION:
A JOURNAL
OF THE
PILGRIMS OF
PLYMOUTH

A JOURNEY TO
PACKANOKIK, THE
HABITATION OF
THE GREAT KING
MASSASOIT: AS
ALSO OUR
MESSAGE, THE
ANSWER AND
ENTERTAINMENT
WE HAD OF HIM

not knowing how our corn might prosper, we could no longer give them such entertainment as we had done, and as we desired still to do. Yet if he would be pleased to come himself, or any special friend of his desired to see us, coming from him they should be welcome. And to the end we might know them from others, our governor had sent him a copper chain; desiring if any messenger should come from him to us, we might know him by bringing it with him, and hearken and give credit to his message accordingly; also requesting him that such as have skins[3] should bring them to us, and that he would hinder the multitude from oppressing us with them. And whereas, at our first arrival at Pamet,[4] called by us Cape Cod, we found there corn buried in the ground, and finding no inhabitants, but some graves of dead new buried, took the corn, resolving, if ever we could hear of any that had right thereunto, to make satisfaction to the full for it; yet since we understand the owners thereof were fled for fear of us, our desire was either to pay them with the like quantity of corn, English meal, or any other commodities we had, to pleasure them withal; requesting him that some one of his men might signify so much unto them, and we would content him for his pains. And last of all, our governor requested one favor of him, which was that he would exchange some of their corn for seed with us, that we might make trail which best agreed with the soil where we live.

With these presents and message we set forward the 10th June,[5] about nine o'clock in the morning, our guide resolving that night to rest at Namaschet,[6] a town under Massasoit, and conceived by us to be very near, because the inhabitants flocked so thick upon every slight occasion amongst us; but we found it to be some fifteen English miles. On the way we found some ten or twelve men, women, and children, which had pestered us till we were weary of them, perceiving that (as the manner of them all is) where victual is easiest to be got, there they live, especially in the summer; by reason whereof, our bay affording many lobsters, they resort every spring-tide thither; and now returned with us to Namaschet. Thither we came about three o'clock after noon, the inhabitants entertaining us with joy, in the best manner they could, giving us a kind of bread called by them *maizium,*[7] and the spawn of shads, which then they got in abundance, insomuch as they gave us spoons to eat them. With these they boiled musty acorns[8]; but of the shads we eat heartily. After this they desired one of our men to shoot at a crow, complaining what damage they sustained in their corn by them; who shooting some fourscore[9] off and killing, they much admired at it, as other shots on other occasions.

After this, Tisquantum told us we should hardly in one day reach Packanokik,[10] moving us to go some eight miles further, where we should find more store and better victuals than there. Being willing to hasten our journey, we went and came thither at sunsetting, where we found many of the Namascheucks (they so calling the

---

3. "Beaver and other skins for the furriers." (Dexter, p. 100) There were plenty of skins available, as John Smith had noted seven years earlier.

4. Pamet.

5. The date is doubtless incorrect, for June 10/20, 1621 was the Sabbath. Bradford and N. Morton use the date July 2/12, 1621, which was a Monday and is undoubtedly correct.

6. Nemasket. The spot designated here is in present-day *Middleboro.* Captain Dermer was here in 1619.

7. Bread made from maize or Indian corn.

8. Boiled dried acorns which the Pilgrims first tasted the previous winter.

9. The word *feet* or paces is missing here.

10. Pokanoket is the generally accepted spelling.

MOURT'S
RELATION:
A JOURNAL
OF THE
PILGRIMS OF
PLYMOUTH

A JOURNEY TO
PACKANOKIK, THE
HABITATION OF
THE GREAT KING
MASSASOIT: AS
ALSO OUR
MESSAGE, THE
ANSWER AND
ENTERTAINMENT
WE HAD OF HIM

men of Nemasket) fishing upon a weir[11] which they had made on a river which belonged to them, where they caught abundance of bass. These welcomed us also, gave us of their fish, and we them of our victuals, not doubting but we should have enough where'er we came. There we lodged in the open fields, for houses they had none, though they spent the most of the summer there. The head of this river is reported to be not far from the place of our abode.[12] Upon it are and have been many towns, it being a good length. The ground is very good on both sides, it being for the most part cleared. Thousands of men have lived there, which died in a great plague not long since; and pity it was and is to see so many goodly fields, and so well seated, without men to dress and manure the same. Upon this river dwelleth Massasoit. It cometh into the sea at the Narrohigganset[13] bay, where the Frenchmen so much use. A ship may go many miles up it, as the savages report, and a shallop to the head of it; but so far as we saw, we are sure a shallop may. But to return to our journey.

The next morning[14] we broke our fast, took our leave, and departed; being then accompanied with some six savages. Having gone about six miles by the river side, at a known shoal place,[15] it being low water, they spake to us to put off our breeches, for we must wade through. Here let me not forget the valor and courage of some of the savages on the opposite side of the river; for there were remaining alive only two men, both aged, especially the one, being above threescore. These two, espying a company of men entering the river, ran very swiftly and low in the grass to meet us at the bank; where, with shrill voices and great courage, standing charged upon us with their bows, they demanded what we were, supposing us to be enemies, and thinking to take advantage of us in the water. But seeing we were friends, they welcomed us with such food as they had, and we bestowed a small bracelet of beads on them. Thus far we are sure the tide ebbs and flows.

Having here again refreshed ourselves, we proceeded in our journey, the weather being very hot for travel; yet the country so well watered, that a man could scarce be dry, but he should have a spring at hand to cool his thirst, beside small rivers in abundance. But the savages will not willingly drink but at a spring-head. When we came to any small brook, where no bridge was, two of them desired to carry us through of their own accords; also, fearing we were or would be weary, offered to carry our pieces; also, if we would lay off any of our clothes, we should have them carried; and as the one of them had found special kindness from one of the messengers, and the other savage from the other, so they showed their thankfulness accordingly in affording us all help and furtherance in the journey.

As we passed along, we observed that there were few places by the river but had been inhabited; by reason whereof much ground was clear, save of weeds, which grew higher than our heads. There is much good timber, both oak, walnut tree, fir, beech, and exceeding great chestnut trees. The country, in respect of the lying of it, is both champaign and hilly, like many places in England. In some places it is very

---

11. In the original this is spelled *wear* and is so pronounced in the area. This is probably the Old Indian Weir near Titicut, in North Middleboro, about three miles southwest of the junction of the Nemasket and Taunton Rivers. Taunton, Massachusetts, has an area called Weir Village, pronounced *ware*.

12. One branch of the Titicut, the Winetuxet, rises in Plympton and Carver, about six miles from Plymouth.

13. Narragansett Bay.

14. Tuesday, July 3/13, 1621.

15. This crossing-place is a *Squawbetty* or Squabetty in the village of East Taunton about 3 ½ miles east by south of Taunton Green. This is about six miles below Old Indian Weir.

MOURT'S
RELATION:
A JOURNAL
OF THE
PILGRIMS OF
PLYMOUTH

A JOURNEY TO
PACKANOKIK, THE
HABITATION OF
THE GREAT KING
MASSASOIT: AS
ALSO OUR
MESSAGE, THE
ANSWER AND
ENTERTAINMENT
WE HAD OF HIM

rocky, both above ground and in it; and though the country be wild and overgrown with woods, yet the trees stand not thick, but a man may well ride a horse amongst them.[16]

Passing on at length, one of the company, an Indian, espied a man, and told the rest of it. We asked them if they feared any. They told us that if they were Narrohig-ganset men, they would not trust them.[17] Whereat we called for our pieces, and bid them not to fear; for though they were twenty, we two alone would not care for them. But they hailing him, he proved a friend, and had only two women with him. Their baskets were empty; but they fetched water in their bottles, so that we drank with them and departed. After we met another man, with other two women, which had been at rendezvous by the salt water; and their baskets were full of roasted crab fishes and other dried shell fish, of which they gave us; and we eat and drank with them, and gave each of the women a string of beads, and departed.

After we came to a town of Massasoit's,[18] where we eat oysters and other fish. From thence we went to Packanokick;[19] but Massasoit was not at home. There we stayed, he being sent for. When news was brought of his coming, our guide Tisquan-tum requested that at our meeting we would discharge our pieces. But one of us going about to charge his piece, the women and children, through fear to see him take up his piece, ran away, and could not be pacified till he laid it down again; who afterward were better informed by our interpreter. Massasoit being come, we discharged our pieces and saluted him; who, after their manner, kindly welcomed us, and took us into his house, and set us down by him; where, having delivered our foresaid message and presents, and having put the coat on his back and the chain about his neck, he was not a little proud to behold himself, and his men also to see their king so bravely attired.

For answer to our message, he told us we were welcome, and he would gladly continue that peace and friendship which was between him and us; and, for his men, they should no more pester us as they had done; also, that he would send to Pamet, and would help us with corn for seed, according to our request.

This being done, his men gathered near to him, to whom he turned himself and made a great speech; they sometimes interposing, and, as it were, confirming and applauding him in that he said. The meaning whereof was, as far as we could learn, thus: Was not he Massasoit, commander of the country about them? Was not such a town his, and the people of it? And should they not bring their skins unto us? To which they answered, they were his, and would be at peace with us, and bring their skins to us. After this manner he named at least thirty places, and their answer was as aforesaid to every one; so that as it was delightful, it was tedious unto us.

This being ended, he lighted tobacco for us, and fell to discoursing of England and of the King's Majesty, marvelling that he would live without a wife.[20] Also he

---

16. Several seventeenth century writers noted that the Indians frequently burned stands of trees to create paths and often got rid of undergrowth by burning.

17. Massasoit and the Narragansetts were at war.

18. This was probably Mattapoisett, now know as *Gardner's Neck* in Swansea. This should not be confused with another Mattapoiset along the coast about thirty-five miles to the east.

19. Several writers have proved that while Pokanoket was the name given to the Wampanoog Territory around Barrington, Warren, and Bristol, R.I., this Indian village was *Sowams,* built around a spring still called Massasoit's Spring in Warren, R.I.

20. James I's wife, Anne of Denmark, died on March 2, 1619.

MOURT'S
RELATION:
A JOURNAL
OF THE
PILGRIMS OF
PLYMOUTH

A JOURNEY TO
PACKANOKIK, THE
HABITATION OF
THE GREAT KING
MASSASOIT: AS
ALSO OUR
MESSAGE, THE
ANSWER AND
ENTERTAINMENT
WE HAD OF HIM

talked of the Frenchmen, bidding us not to suffer them to come to Narrohigganset, for it was King James's country, and he was also King James's man. Late it grew, but victuals he offered none; for indeed he had not any, being he came so newly home. So we desired to go to rest. He laid us on the bed with himself and his wife, they at the one end and we at the other, it being only planks laid a foot from the ground and a thin mat upon them.[21] Two more of his chief men, for want of room, pressed by and upon us; so that we were weary more of our lodging than of our journey.

The next day, being Thursday,[22] many of their *sachems,* or petty governors, came to see us, and many of their men also. There they went to their manner of games for skins and knives.[23] There we challenged them to shoot with them for skins, but they durst not; only they desired to see one of us shoot at a mark, who shooting with hail-shot, they wondered to see the mark so full of holes.

About one o'clock Massasoit brought two fishes that he had shot; they were like bream, but three times so big, and better meat.[24] These being boiled, there were at least forty looked for share in them; the most eat of them. This meal only we had in two nights and a day; and had not one of us bought a partridge,[25] we had taken our journey fasting. Very importunate he was to have us stay with them longer. But we desired to keep the Sabbath at home; and feared we should either be light-headed for want of sleep, for what with bad lodging, the savages' barbarous singing, (for they used to sing themselves asleep,) lice and fleas within doors, and mosquitoes without, we could hardly sleep all the time of our being there; we much fearing that if we should stay any longer, we should not be able to recover home for want of strength. So that on the Friday morning, before sunrising,[26] we took our leave and departed, Massasoit being both grieved and ashamed that he could no better entertain us; and retaining Tisquantum to send from place to place to procure truck for us, and appointing another, called Tokamahamon, in his place, whom we had found faithful before and after upon all occasions.

At this town of Massasoit's, where we before ate,[27] we were again refreshed with a little fish, and bought about a handful of meal of their parched corn, which was very precious at that time of the year, and a small string of dried shellfish, as big as oysters.[28] The latter we gave to the six savages that accompanied us, keeping the meal for ourselves. When we drank, we eat each a spoonful of it with a pipe of tobacco, instead of other victuals; and of this also we could not but give them so long as it

---

21. Thomas Morton in his *New English Canaan* wrote, "Their lodging is made in three places of the house about the fire. They lie upon planks, commonly about a foot or eighteen inches above the ground, raised upon rails that are borne up upon forks. They lay mats under them, and coats of deer's skins, otters', beavers', racoons', and of bears', hiding all which they have dressed and converted into good leather, with the hair on, for their coverings; and in this manner they lie as warm as they desire." Since it was summer, warmth should not have been a problem. The paragraph, though, is another example of the Pilgrims' grim humor.

22. Thursday, July 5/15, 1621.

23. Several games played by Indians were noted by Roger Williams. One was a game played with "strong rushes," and another was a game played by tossing painted stones in a bay. We don't know whether the Pilgrims were about to gamble at this point, but the game they proposed was one that they could not lose.

24. Fessenden in his *History of Warren, R.I.*, suggests that these were probably "bass, as those fish swim near the surface." Young (p. 211) thinks the fish might have been tataug, a fish still frequently caught in the area.

25. Probably *bought* should read *brought.*

26. Friday, July 6/16, 1621.

27. Again at Mattapoisett or Gardner's Neck in Swansea.

28. Clams or quahaugs.

57

MOURT'S
RELATION:
A JOURNAL
OF THE
PILGRIMS OF
PLYMOUTH

A JOURNEY TO
PACKANOKIK, THE
HABITATION OF
THE GREAT KING
MASSASOIT: AS
ALSO OUR
MESSAGE, THE
ANSWER AND
ENTERTAINMENT
WE HAD OF HIM

lasted. Five miles they led us to a house out of the way in hope of victuals; but we found nobody there, and so were but worse able to return home. That night we reached to the weir[29] where we lay before; but the Namascheucks were returned, so that we had no hope of any thing there. One of the savages had shot a shad in the water, and a small squirrel, as big as a rat, called a *neuxis;*[30] the one half of either he gave us, and after went to the weir to fish. From hence we wrote to Plymouth, and sent Tokamahamon before to Namasket, willing him from thence to send another, that he might meet us with Namasket. Two men now only remained with us; and it pleased God to give them good store of fish, so that we were well refreshed. After supper we went to rest, and they to fishing again. More they gat, and fell to eating afresh, and retained sufficient ready roast for all our breakfasts.

About two o'clock in the morning,[31] arose a great storm of wind, rain, lightning, and thunder, in such violent manner that we could not keep in our fire; and had the savages not roasted fish when we were asleep, we had set forward fasting; for the rain still continued with great violence, even the whole day through, till we came within two miles of home. Being wet and weary, at length we came to Namaschet. There we refreshed ourselves, giving gifts to all such as had showed us any kindness. Amongst others, one of the six that came with us from Packanokick, having before this on the way unkindly forsaken us, marvelled we gave him nothing, and told us what he had done for us. We also told him of some discourtesies he offered us, whereby he deserved nothing. Yet we gave him a small trifle; whereupon he offered us tobacco. But the house being full of people, we told them he stole some by the way, and if it were of that, we would not take it; for we would not receive that which was stolen, upon any terms; if we did, our God would be angry with us, and destroy us. This abashed him, and gave the rest great content. But, at our departure, he would needs carry him[32] on his back through a river whom he had formerly in some sort abused. Fain they would have had us to lodge there all night, and wondered we would set forth again in such weather. But, God be praised, we came safe home that night, though wet, weary, and surbated.[33]

---

29. In *Titicut.* See notes 11-12.
30. Evidently this was the Indian name for the little colored squirrel. Dexter identifies it as probably the *Sciurus leucotis* or *Sciurus striatus.*
31. Saturday, July 7/17, 1621.
32. *Him* refers to Edward Winslow, the author of this work.
33. Surbated = bruised, harassed, fatigued.

Portrait of Edward Winslow, Painted in
London, 1651, Probably by Robert Walker
Courtesy of the Pilgrim Society

A Voyage Made by Ten of Our Men to the Kingdom of Nauset,[1] to Seek a Boy[2] that had Lost Himself in the Woods: With Such Accidents as Befell Us in that Voyage

The 11th of June[3] we set forth, the weather being very fair. But ere we had been long at sea, there arose a storm of wind and rain, with much lightning and thunder, insomuch that a spout arose not far from us. But, God be praised, it dured not long, and we put in that night for harbor at a place called Cummaquid,[4] where we had some hope to find the boy. Two savages were in the boat with us. The one was Tisquantum, our interpreter; the other Tokamahamon,[5] a special friend. It being night before we came in, we anchored in the midst of the Bay, where we were dry at a low water. In the morning we espied savages seeking lobsters, and sent our two interpreters to speak with them, the channel being between them; where they told them what we were, and for what we were come, willing them not at all to fear us, for we

---

1. The Indian name for Eastham on Cape Cod. This portion, too, would appear to be the work of Edward Winslow.

2. The boy was John Billington, whose younger brother had almost blown up the *Mayflower* in Provincetown harbor, December 5/15, 1620. Evidently Massasoit had sent word that young Billington was at Nauset.

3. Monday, June 11/21, 1621 is indicated but this date is unlikely. Prince (p. 192) notes that "Mourt's *Relation*, and *Purchas* from it, places this on June 11. But this date being inconsistent with several hints in the foregoing and following stories, I keep to Governor Bradford's original manuscript, and place it between the end of July and the 13th of August." Bradford writes, "About the latter end of this month (July), one John Billington lost himself in the woods, and wandered up and down some five days, living on berries and what he could find. At length he *light* on an Indian plantation twenty miles south of this place, called Manomet; they conveyed him further off among those people that had set upon the English when they were coasting whilst the ship lay at the cape. . . ." (pp. 97-98)

4. Cummaquid is the Indian name for Barnstable Harbor. Young (p. 215) writes that "it is formed by a neck of land about half a mile wide, called Sandy Neck, which projects from Sandwich on the north shore, and runs east almost the length of the town. The harbor is about a mile wide, and four miles long. The tide rises in it from 10 to 14 feet. It has a bar running off northeast from the neck several miles, which prevents the entrance of large ships."

5. Tokamahamon had been assigned by Massasoit to help Winslow and Hopkins at Sowams early on July 6/16.

MOURT'S
RELATION:
A JOURNAL
OF THE
PILGRIMS OF
PLYMOUTH

A VOYAGE
MADE BY TEN
OF OUR MEN TO
THE KINGDOM
OF NAUSET, TO
SEEK A BOY
THAT HAD LOST
HIMSELF IN THE
WOODS: WITH
SUCH ACCIDENTS
AS BEFELL US IN
THAT VOYAGE

would not hurt them. Their answer was, that the boy was well, but he was at Nauset; yet since we were there, they desired us to come ashore, and eat with them; which, as soon as our boat floated, we did, and went six ashore, having four pledges for them in the boat. They brought us to their sachem, or governor, whom they call Iyanough,[6] a man not exceeding twenty-six years of age, but very personable, gentle, courteous, and fair conditioned, indeed not like a savage, save for his attire. His entertainment was answerable to his parts, and his cheer plentiful and various.

One thing was very grievous unto us at this place. There was an old woman, whom we judged to be no less than a hundred years old, which came to see us, because she never saw English; yet could not behold us without breaking forth into great passion, weeping and crying excessively. We demanding the reason of it, they told us she had three sons, who, when Master Hunt[7] was in these parts, went aboard his ship to trade with him, and he carried them captives into Spain, (for Tisquantum at that time was carried away also,) by which means she was deprived of the company of her children in her old age. We told them we were sorry that any Englishman should give them that offense, that Hunt was a bad man, and that all the English that heard of it condemned him for the same; but for us, we would not offer them any such injury, though it would gain us all the skins in the country. So we gave her some small trifles, which somewhat appeased her.

After dinner we took boat for Nauset, Iyanough and two of his men accompanying us. Ere we came to Nauset, the day and tide were almost spent, insomuch as we could not go in with our shallop;[8] but the sachem or governor of Cummaquid went ashore, and his men with him. We also sent Tisquantum to tell Aspinet,[9] the sachem of Nauset, wherefore we came. The savages here came very thick amongst us, and were earnest with us to bring in our boat. But we neither well could, nor yet desired to do it, because we had less cause to trust them, being they only had formerly made an assault upon us in the same place,[10] in time of our winter discovery for habitation. And indeed it was no marvel they did so; for howsoever, through snow or otherwise, we saw no houses, yet we were in the midst of them.

When our boat was aground, they came very thick; but we stood therein upon our guard, not suffering any to enter except two, the one being of Manamoick,[11] and one of those whose corn we had formerly found. We promised him restitution, and desired him either to come to Patuxet for satisfaction, or else we would bring them so much corn again. He promised to come. We used him very kindly for the present. Some few skins we got there, but not many.

After sunset, Aspinet came with a great train, and brought the boy with him, one

---

6. Iyanough, who was highly regarded by Winslow at this time, did not remain friendly with the Pilgrims. In 1623 the Indians formed a conspiracy to kill the English, and Iyanough was involved. Massasoit revealed the plot, and Iyanough, terrifed at the prospect of dire punishment by the English, fled in the swamps where he died of starvation or disease.

7. The name of Captain Thomas Hunt "has come down to us loaded with deserved infamy, as the first kidnapper and slave dealer on the coast of North America." (Young, p. 186) Bradford and John Smith are agreed that he sold at least 27 Indian slaves from the Plymouth and Nauset area at £20 a man.

8. At Eastham the water is very shoal. (Young, p. 216)

9. Aspinet's tribe, although not part of the Wampanoags, was nevertheless subordinate to Massasoit. Dexter writes (p. 114) that the "meagre record indicates that Aspinet perished miserably as Iyanough did."

10. At the time of the first landing of the Pilgrims in November, 1620.

11. There are many spellings of this including Monomoyick, Manamoyik, Monamey, etc. The area is present-day Chatham, the southern extremity of Cape Cod.

bearing him through the water.[12] He had not less than a hundred with him; the half whereof came to the shallop side unarmed with him; the other stood aloof with their bows and arrows. There he delivered us the boy, behung with beads, and made peace with us;[13] we bestowing a knife on him, and likewise on another that first entertained the boy and brought him thither. So they departed from us.

MOURT'S RELATION: A JOURNAL OF THE PILGRIMS OF PLYMOUTH

A VOYAGE MADE BY TEN OF OUR MEN TO THE KINGDOM OF NAUSET, TO SEEK A BOY THAT HAD LOST HIMSELF IN THE WOODS: WITH SUCH ACCIDENTS AS BEFELL US IN THAT VOYAGE

Here we understood that the Narrohigganstets had spoiled some of Massasoit's men, and taken him. This struck some fear in us, because the colony was so weakly guarded, the strength thereof being abroad.[14] But we set forth with resolution to make the best haste home we could; yet the wind being contrary, having scarce any fresh water left, and at least sixteen leagues home,[15] we put in again for the shore. There we met with Iyanough, the sachem of Cummaquid, and the most of his town, both men, women and children with him. He, being still willing to gratify us, took a runlet,[16] and led our men in the dark a great way for water, but could find none good; yet brought such as there was on his neck with them. In the mean time the women joined hand in hand, singing and dancing before the shallop, the men also showing all the kindness they could, Iyanough himself taking a bracelet from about his neck and hanging it upon one of us.

Again we set out, but to small purpose; for we got but little homeward. Our water also was very brackish, and not to be drunk. The next morning Iyanough espied us again, and ran after us. We, being resolved to go to Cummaquid again to water, took him into the shallop, whose entertainment was not inferior unto the former.

The soil at Nauset and here is alike, even and sandy, not so good for corn as where we are. Ships may safely ride in either harbor. In the summer they abound with fish. Being now watered, we put forth again, and by God's providence came safely home that night.

---

12. Bradford wrote of the Billington boy, "He had wandered five days, lived on berries, then light of an Indian plantation, twenty miles south of us, called Manomet (Sandwich) and they conveyed him to the people who first assaulted us." (Quoted in Prince, *New England Chronology*, p. 192).

13. Bradford writes that "Those people also came and made their peace; and they gave full satisfaction to those whose corn they had founded and taken when they were at Cape Cod."

14. The Pilgrims in making this expedition left Plymouth defenseless. Young notes (pp. 217-218) that "There were ten men in this expedition. At the same time, according to the dates of this and the previous paper, Winslow and Hopkins were absent on their expedition to Pokonoket, leaving only seven men at the Plantation, the whole number surviving at this time being nineteen."

15. A slight exaggeration. The distance from Eastham to Plymouth is about twelve leagues (35 miles).

16. Runlet = rundlet = a small barrel containing from 3 to 20 gallons.

"The First Religious Service of the Pilgrims"
After a Painting by Johan Gorg Schwartze of Amsterdam (1859)
Courtesy of the Pilgrim Society

A Journey to the Kingdom of Namaschet,[1] in Defence of the Great King Massasoit Against the Narrohiggansets, and to Revenge the Supposed Death of Our Interpreter, Tisquantum

At our return from Nauset we found it true that Massasoit was put from his country by the Narragansetts.[2] Word also was brought unto us that Coubatant,[3] a petty sachem or governor under Massasoit, whom they ever feared to be too conversant with the Narragansetts, was at Nemasket; who sought to draw the hearts of Massasoit's subjects from him; speaking also disdainfull of us, storming at the peace between Nauset, Cummaquid and us, and at Tisquantum, the worker of it; also at Tokamahomon and one Hobbamock, two Indians, our allies,[4] one of which he would treacherously have murdered a little before, being a special and trusty man of Massasoit's. Tokamahamon went to him, but the other two would not; yet put their lives in their hands, privately went to see if they could hear of their king, and lodging at Namaschet were discovered to Coubatant, who set a guard to beset the house, and took Tisquantum; for he had said if he were dead, the English had lost their tongue. Hobbamock, seeing that Tisquantum was taken, and Coubatant held a knife at his breast, being a strong and stout man, brake from them and came to New Plymouth, full of fear and sorrow for Tisquantum, whom he thought to be slain.

Upon this news the company assembled together, and resolved on the morrow to send ten men armed to Namaschet, and Hobbamock for their guide, to revenge the supposed death of Tisquantum on Coubatant, our bitter enemy, and to retain

---

1. Namaschet (Nemasket) is the area around present-day Middleboro and Lakeville, Massachusetts.

2. Bradford covers this incident in some detail in *Of Plimoth Plantation*.

3. Bradford writes his name as *Corbitant*. His headquarters were at Mattapoisett (Gardner's Neck) in present day Swansea.

4. In the original printing (1622) *our allies* appears as "or Lemes," obviously a typographical error.

MOURT'S
RELATION:
A JOURNAL
OF THE
PILGRIMS OF
PLYMOUTH

A JOURNEY TO
THE KINGDOM
OF NAMASCHET,
IN DEFENCE OF
THE GREAT KING
MASSASOIT
AGAINST THE
NARROHIGGAN-
SETS, AND TO
REVENGE THE
SUPPOSED
DEATH OF OUR
INTERPRETER,
TISQUANTUM

Nepeof,[5] another sachem or governor, who was of this confederacy, till we heard what was become of our friend Massasoit.

On the morrow[6] we set out ten[7] men, armed, who took their journey as aforesaid; but the day proved very wet. When we supposed we were within three or four miles of Namaschet,[8] we went out of the way, and stayed there till night; because we would not be discovered. There we consulted what to do; and thinking best to beset the house at midnight, each was appointed his task by the Captain,[9] all men encouraging one another to the utmost of their power. By night our guide lost his way, which much discouraged our men, being we were wet, and weary of our arms. But one[10] of our men, having been before at Nemasket, brought us into the way again.

Before we came to the town, we sat down and ate such as our knapsacks afforded. That being done, we threw them aside, and all such things as might hinder us, and so went on to beset the house, according to our last resolution. Those that entered demanded if Coubatant were not there; but fear had bereft the savages of speech. We charged them not to stir; for if Coubatant were not there, we would not meddle with them. If he were, we came principally for him, to be avenged on him for the supposed death of Tisquantum, and other matters; but, howsoever, we would not at all hurt their women or children. Notwithstanding, some of them pressed out at a private door and escaped, but with some wounds.

At length, preceiving our principal ends, they told us Coubatant was returned with all his train, and that Tisquantum was yet living and in the town; offering some tobacco, other such as they had to eat. In this hurly-burly we discharged two pieces at random, which much terrified all the inhabitants, except Tisquantum and Tokamahamon; who, though they knew not our end in coming, yet assured them of our honesty, that we would not hurt them. Those boys that were in the house, seeing our care of women, often cried "Neen squaes!"[11] that is to say, "I am a woman";[12] the women also hanging upon Hobbamock, calling him *towam*, that is *friend*.[13] But, to be short, we kept them we had, and made them make a fire, that we might see to search the house. In the mean time, Hobbamock gat on the top of the house, and called Tisquantum and Tokamahamon, which came unto us accompanied with others, some armed, and others naked. Those that had bows and arrows, we took them away, promising them again when it was day. The house we took, for our better safeguard, but released those we had taken, manifesting whom we came for and wherefore.

On the next morning we marched into the midst of the town, and went to the

---

5. This Indian's name, *Nepeof*, does not appear in any other record of the era.

6. Tuesday, August 14/24, 1621.

7. Bradford says that "it was resolved to send the Captain and 14 men well armed, and to go and fall upon them in the night."

8. Dexter (p. 121) writes that "Corbitant seems to have had a temporary summer residence at what is now known as Muttock Hill, in Middleborough, about three-quarters of a mile n.n.w. of the village of the Four Corners," near the site of the present Oliver Mill Park on Route 44.

9. Miles Standish.

10. Young (pp. 220-221) states that "Either Winslow or Hopkins, who stopped at Namesket in going and returning from Pokonoket, in July. If it was Winslow, he may reasonably be considered the writer of this narrative."

11. "This is correct Indian in the Massachusetts and Narragansett dialects." (Young, p. 221)

12. According to the purists "Neen Squaes!" means "I am a girl."

13. There seems to be no authority for the word *towam* meaning *friend*.

house of Tisquantum to breakfast. Thither came all whose hearts were upright towards us; but all Coubatant's faction were fled away. There, in the midst of them, we manifested again our intendment, assuring them, that although Coubatant had now escaped us, yet there was no place should secure him and his from us, if he continued his threatening of us, and provoking others against us, who had kindly entertained him, and never intended evil towards him till he now so justly deserved it. Moreover, if Massasoit did not return in safely from Narrohigganset, or if hereafter he should make any insurrection against him or offer violence to Tisquantum, Hobbamock, or any of Massasoit's subjects, we would revenge it upon him, to the over throw of him and his. As for those (who) were wounded, we were sorry for it, though themselves procured it in not staying in the house, at our command; yet if they would return home with us, our surgeon[14] should heal them.

At this offer, one man and a woman that were wounded went home with us; Tisquantum and many other known friends accompanying us, and offering all help that might be by carriage of any thing we had, to ease us. So that by God's good providence we safely returned home the morrow night after we set forth.

MOURT'S RELATION: A JOURNAL OF THE PILGRIMS OF PLYMOUTH

A JOURNEY TO THE KINGDOM OF NAMASCHET, IN DEFENCE OF THE GREAT KING MASSASOIT AGAINST THE NARROHIGGAN-SETS, AND TO REVENGE THE SUPPOSED DEATH OF OUR INTERPRETER, TISQUANTUM

14. Their physician was Samuel Fuller.

"The First Thanksgiving"
by Jennie A. Brownscombe
Courtesy of the Pilgrim Society

A Relation of Our Voyage to the Massachusetts,[1] and What Happened There

It seemed good to the company in general, that though the Massachusetts had often threatened us, (as we were informed,) yet we should go amongst them, partly to see the country, partly to make peace with them, and partly to procure their truck. For these ends the governors chose ten men, fit for the purpose, and sent Tisquantum and two other savages to bring us to speech with the people and interpret for us.

We set out about midnight, the tide then serving for us.[2] We supposing it to be nearer than it is, thought to be there the next morning betimes; but it proved well near twenty leagues from New Plymouth.[3] We came into the bottom of the bay;[4] but being late, we anchored and lay in the shallop, not having seen any of the people. The next morning we put in for the shore. There we found many lobsters, that had been gathered together by the savages, which we made ready under a cliff.[5] The Captain[6] set two sentinels behind the cliff, to the landward, to secure the shallop, and taking a guide with him and four of our company, went to see the inhabitants; where they met a woman coming for her lobsters. They told her of them, and contented her for them. She told them where the people were. Tisquantum went to them; the rest returned, having direction which way to bring the shallop to them.

The sachem or governor of this place is called Obbatinewat; and though he lives in the bottom of the Massachusetts Bay,[7] yet he is under Massasoit. He used us very

---

1. The Massachusetts tribe inhabited the area around Boston bay. Both the Indian tribe and the area derived their name from the Blue Hills in Milton.

2. Tuesday, September 18/28, 1621. Bradford writes in his *Of Plimoth Plantation*: "After this, the 18 of September, they sent out their shallop to the Massachusetts with 10 men and Squanto for their guide and interpreter to discover and view the bay and trade with the natives; the which they performed and found kind entertainment."

3. This is an exaggeration as the distance from Plymouth to Boston by water is about forty-four miles.

4. Dexter (p. 125) indicates, "That is, run in by Point Allerton into Lighthouse Channel." Point Allerton is at the head-land of Nantasket.

5. Young (p. 125) believes this to be Copp's Hill in present-day Boston's North End. Dexter, using later information, concludes "that they struck directly, a little south of west across Quincy bay, to the nearest shore and that the 'cliff' was that pile of rocks known as 'the chapel' at the northeast extremity of the peninsula of Squantum." This editor agrees with Dexter's conclusion. It is generally assumed that Squantum is named in honor of Squanto or Tisquantum, who accompanied the Pilgrims on this trip.

6. Miles Standish.

7. Young (p. 225) points out that "By Massachusetts Bay was formerly understood only the inner bay, from Nahant to Point Allerton. Thus Governor Winthrop speaks of going from Salem to Massachusetts."

MOURT'S
RELATION:
A JOURNAL
OF THE
PILGRIMS OF
PLYMOUTH

A RELATION OF
OUR VOYAGE TO
THE MASSACHUS-
ETTS, AND WHAT
HAPPENED THERE

kindly. He told us he durst not then remain in any settled place for fear of the Taren-tines.[8] Also the squaw sachem,[9] or Massachusetts queen, was an enemy to him.

We told him of divers sachems that had acknowledged themselves to be King James's men,[10] and if he also would submit himself, we would be his safeguard from his enemies; which he did, and went along with us to bring us to the squaw sachem. Again we crossed the bay, which is very large, and hath at least fifty islands in it;[11] but the certain number is not known to the inhabitants. Night it was before we came to that side of the bay where this people were. On shore the savages went, but found nobody. That night also we rode at anchor aboard the shallop.

On the morrow[12] we went ashore,[13] all but two men, and marched in arms up in the country. Having gone three miles we came to a place where corn had been newly gathered, a house pulled down, and the people gone. A mile from hence, Nanepashemet, their king, in his life-term had lived.[14] His house was not like others, but a scaffold was largely built, with poles[15] and planks, some six foot from (the) ground, and the house upon that, being situated on the top of a hill.[16]

Not far from hence, in a bottom[17] we came to a fort, built by their deceased king; the manner thus. There were poles, some thirty or forty feet long, stuck in the ground, as thick as they could be set one by another; and with these they enclosed a ring some forty or fifty feet over;[18] a trench, breast high, was digged on each side; one way there was to go into it with a bridge. In the midst of this palisado stood the frame of a house, wherein, being dead, he lay buried.[19]

About a mile from hence, we came to such another, but seated on the top of a hill. Here Nanepashemet was killed, none dwelling in it since the time of his death. At this place we stayed, and sent two savages to look (for) the inhabitants, and to inform them of our ends in coming, that they might not be fearful of us. Within a mile of this place they found the women of the place together, with their corn on heaps,

8. The Tarentines (Tarrateens, Tarrenteins) lived on the Penobscot River in Maine.

9. Both Young (p. 225) and Dexter (p. 126) believe that she was the widow of *Nanepashemet.* She later married *Webbacowet,* the great medicine-man of the Massachusetts. See note 14 below.

10. The reference is to the nine sachems who had declared themselves to be loyal subjects of King James at Plymouth a week or so earlier, September 13/23, 1621.

11. The number is not an exaggeration although several of the islands known in the seventeenth century have been wasted away. John Smith in his *Description of New England* (1616) wrote, "The country of the Massachusetts is the paradise of all those parts; for here are many isles all planted with corn, groves, mulberries, and savage gardens."

12. Friday, September 21/October 1, 1621.

13. Young (p. 226), who believed that they first landed at Copp's Hill, places this landing at Squantum. Dexter, with whom this editor agrees, feels that "They seem to have crossed from Quincy over to what is now Charlestown." (p. 127)

14. Nanepashemet, a powerful sachem, lived at Lynn until the "great war with the *Taretines.*" "He then retreated to Medford, where he built him a house on Rock Hill. He was killed by the Taretines in 1619." (Dexter, p. 127)

15. In the original *pools.*

16. Young (p. 226) believes this to be Milton Hill or some one of the Blue Hills. It is actually Rock Hill in Medford. See note 14 above.

17. Near Mystic Pond in Medford.

18. Young notes (p. 227) that "This corresponds exactly with the engraving of the Pequot Fort in Underhill's *News from America,* printed in London in 1638, and reprinted in *Mass. Hist. Coll.* xxvi, 23."

19. Dexter adds, "An Indian skeleton was exhumed in West Medford, Mass., 21 Oct, 1802, a short distance s.e. from Mystic Pond, which, partly because there was with it a pipe with a copper mouthpiece, it was thought might be *Nanipashemet's.*"

MOURT'S
RELATION:
A JOURNAL
OF THE
PILGRIMS OF
PLYMOUTH

A RELATION OF
OUR VOYAGE TO
THE MASSACHUS-
ETTS, AND WHAT
HAPPENED THERE

wither we supposed them to be fled for fear of us; and the more, because in divers places they had newly pulled down their houses,[20] and for haste in one place had left some of their corn covered with a mat, and nobody with it.

With much fear they entertained us at first; but seeing our gentle carriage towards them, they took heart and entertained us in the best manner they could, boiling cod and such other things as they had for us. At length, with much sending for, came one of their men, shaking and trembling for fear. But when he saw we intended them no hurt, but came to truck, he promised us his skins also. Of him we inquired for their queen; but it seemed she was far from thence;[21] at least we could not see her.

Here Tisquantum would have had us rifle the savage women, and taken their skins and all such things as might be serviceable for us; for, said he, they are a bad people, and have oft threatened you. But our answer was, were they never so bad, we would not wrong them, or give them any just occasion against us. For their words, we little weighted them; but if they once attempted anything against us, then we would deal far worse than he desired.

Having well spent the day, we returned to the shallop, almost all the women accompanying us to truck, who sold their coats from their backs, and tied boughs about them, but with great shamefacedness,[22] for indeed they are more modest than some of our English women are. We promised them to come again to them, and they us to keep their skins.

Within this bay the savages say there are two rivers;[23] the one whereof we saw, having a fair entrance, but we had no time to discover it. Better harbors for shipping cannot be than here are. At the entrance of the bay are many rocks;[24] and in all likelihood good fishing-ground.[25] Many, yea most of the islands have been inhabited, some being cleared from end to end. But the people are all dead,[26] or removed.

Our victual growing scarce, the wind coming fair, and having a light moon, we set out at evening, and through the goodness of God came safely home before noon the day following.[27]

---

20. Houses were hastily constructed, a few stakes, some branches and mats made up the frame and the enclosure so they could be almost portable.

21. An historian of Concord, Lemuel Shattuck, places her residence in that town.

22. In the original shamefastness.

23. "The Mystic and the Charles, the former of which they saw in their visit to Nanepashemet's house and grave &c." (Dexter, p. 131)

24. "12. The Brewsters, Calf Island, Egg Rock, The Graves, Harding's Rocks, and Tainsford Rocks, keep their places in and around our harbor." (Dexter, p. 131)

25. Young adds, "The neighborhood of these rocks is excellent fishing-ground." (p. 229)

26. They had been wiped out by the pestilence a few years earlier.

27. Saturday, September 22/October 2, 1621.

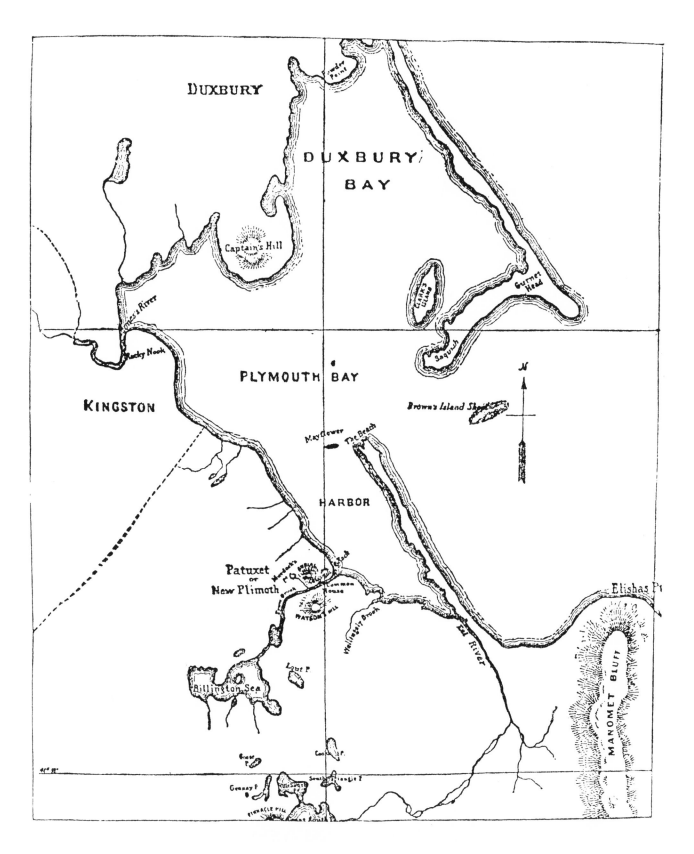

Map of Plymouth and Vicinity
in Dexter's Edition of *Mourt's Relation*

A Letter Sent from New England to a Friend in These Parts,[1] Setting Forth a Brief and True Declaration of the Worth of That Plantation; As Also Certain Useful Directions for Such as Intend a Voyage into Those Parts

Loving and Old Friend,[2]

ALTHOUGH I received no letter from you by this ship,[3] yet forasmuch as I know you expect the performance of my promise, which was, to write unto you truly and faithfully of all things, I have therefore at this time sent unto you accordingly, referring you for further satisfaction to our more large Relations.[4]

You shall understand that in this little time that a few of us have been here,[5] we have built seven dwelling-houses[6] and four for the use of the plantation, and have

---

1. Dexter notes (p. 131) that "This heading was prefixed in England by the party receiving the letter, who was probably the person who published the same, with the 'more large Relations' which accompanied it and to which reference is made. Writing in England, he naturally says 'these' parts."

2. All of the evidence would seem to indicate that the letter was addressed to George Morton. See biographical sketch in introduction.

3. The reference is, of course, to the *Fortune,* which had landed in Plymouth in November and in which this letter and the other accounts were sent to England.

4. The original narrative generally known as *Mourt's Relation* as penned by Bradford and Winslow.

5. Since Winslow's letter is dated December 11/21, 1621 and they had been in Plymouth since December 20/30, 1620, this "little time" amounted to almost one year.

6. The visitor to the present-day replica of Plimoth Plantation must wonder at Winslow's reference to seven houses. The reconstruction is of the 1627 village, six years after this letter was sent. Since half of the original Mayflower settlers had died the first winter, these seven houses should have been enough to care for the remaining passengers in homes of seven or eight persons each.

MOURT'S
RELATION:
A JOURNAL
OF THE
PILGRIMS OF
PLYMOUTH

A LETTER SENT
FROM NEW ENG-
LAND TO A
FRIEND IN
THESE PARTS,
SETTING FORTH A
BRIEF AND TRUE
DECLARATION OF
THE WORTH OF
THAT PLANTA-
TION; AS ALSO
CERTAIN USEFUL
DIRECTIONS FOR
SUCH AS INTEND
A VOYAGE INTO
THOSE PARTS

made preparation for divers others. We set the last spring some twenty acres of Indian corn,[7] and sowed some six acres of barley and pease; and according to the manner of the Indians, we manured our ground with herrings, or rather shads,[8] which we have in great abundance, and take with great ease at our doors.[9] Our corn did prove well; and, God be praised, we had a good increase of Indian corn, and our barley indifferent good, but our pease not worth the gathering, for we feared they were too late sown. They came up very well, and blossomed; but the sun parched them in the blossom.

Our harvest being gotten, our governor[10] sent four men on fowling, that so we might, after a special manner, rejoice together after we had gathered the fruit of our labors.[11] They four in one day killed as much fowl as, with a little help beside, served the company almost a week. At which time, amongst other recreations, we exercised our arms, many of the Indians coming amongst us, and among the rest their greatest king, Massasoit, with some ninety men, whom for three days we entertained and feasted; and they went out and killed five deer,[12] which they brought to the planta-tion, and bestowed on our governor, and upon the captain and others. And although it be not always so plentiful as it was at this time with us, yet by the goodness of God we are so far from want, that we often wish you partakers of our plenty.[13]

We have found the Indians very faithful in their covenant of peace with us, very loving, and ready to pleasure us. We often go to them, and they come to us. Some of us have been fifty miles[14] by land in the country with them, the occasions and rela-tions whereof you shall understand by our general and more full declaration of such things as are worth the noting. Yea, it hath pleased God so to possess the Indians with a fear of us and love unto us, that not only the greatest king amongst them, called Massasoit, but also all the princes and peoples round about us, have either made suit unto us, or been glad of any occasion to make peace with us; so that seven of them at once have sent their messengers to us to that end.[15] Yea, an isle[16] at sea,[17]

---

7. Bradford points out their indebtedness to Squanto as "a great help, showing us how to set, fish, dress, and tend it."

8. Alewives. Thomas Morton in his *New English Canaan* writes, "There is a fish (by some called shads, by some *allizes*), that at the spring of the year pass up the river and spawn in the ponds; and are taken in such multitudes in every river, that hath a pond at the end, that the inhabitants dung their ground with them. You may see 100 acres together set with these fish, every acre taking 1000 of them." The Indians put two or three fish in each cornhill, and when they rotted the fish fertilized the seed corn.

9. "In Town Brook, as the fish thronged it in the spring to go up." (Dexter, p. 132)

10. William Bradford.

11. This was the first Thanksgiving.

12. Young adds, "On this occasion they no doubt feasted on the wild turkey as well as venison." (p. 231)

13. Young points out that "This representation was rather too encouraging, as will be seen hereafter" (p. 232) but Dexter states fairly, "This was written honestly when it was written, though the addition of the *Fortune's* com-pany to theirs, and the necessity of victualling that ship for her return voyage, made them know what famine was in the winter that was just beginning." (p. 134) Of the period after the *Fortune* sailed, Bradford writes, "So they were presently put to half allowance, one as well as another, which began to be hard; but they bore it patiently under hope of supply."

14. The distance from Plymouth to the Pokonoket lands is about forty miles.

15. The document that Winslow refers to is printed in N. Morton's *New England's Memorial*. It states:

September 13, anno Dom. 1621

Know all men by these presents, that we, whose names are underwritten, do acknowledge ourselves to be the loyal subjects of King James, king of Great Britain, France, and Ireland, Defender of the Faith, &c. In witness whereof, and as a testimonial of the same, we have subscribed our names or marks as followeth:

which we never saw, hath also, together with the former, yielded willingly to be under the protection and subject to our sovereign lord King James. So that there is now great peace amongst the Indians themselves, which was not formerly, neither would have been but for us; and we, for our parts, walk as peaceably and safely in the wood as in the highways in England. We entertain them familiarly in our houses, and they as friendly bestowing their venison on us. They are a people without any religion or knowledge of any God,[18] yet very trusty, quick of apprehension, ripe-witted, just. The men and women go naked, only a skin about their middles.

For the temper of the air here, it agreeth well with that in England; and if there be any difference at all, this is somewhat hotter in summer. Some think it to be colder in winter; but I cannot out of experience so say. The air is very clear, and not foggy, as hath been reported. I never in my life remember a more seasonable year that we have here enjoyed; and if we have once but kine,[19] horses, and sheep, I make no question but men might live as contented here as in any part of the world. For fish and fowl, we have great abundance. Fresh cod in the summer is but coarse meat with us. Our bay is full of lobsters[20] all the summer, and affordeth variety of other fish. In September we can take a hogshead of eels in a night, with small labor, and can dig them out of their beds all the winter.[21] We have mussels and othus[22] at our doors. Oysters we have none near, but we can have them brought by the Indians when we will. All the spring-time the earth sendeth forth naturally very good sallet herbs.[23] Here are grapes,[24] white and red, and very sweet and strong also; strawberries, gooseberries, raspis,[25] &c.; plums[26] of three sorts, white,[27] black, and red, being almost as good as a damson; abundance of roses, white, red and damask; single, but very sweet indeed. The country wanteth only industrious men to employ; for it would grieve your hearts if, as I, you had seen so many miles together by goodly

MOURT'S RELATION: A JOURNAL OF THE PILGRIMS OF PLYMOUTH

A LETTER SENT FROM NEW ENGLAND TO A FRIEND IN THESE PARTS, SETTING FORTH A BRIEF AND TRUE DECLARATION OF THE WORTH OF THAT PLANTATION; AS ALSO CERTAIN USEFUL DIRECTIONS FOR SUCH AS INTEND A VOYAGE INTO THOSE PARTS

Ohquamehud,	Chikkatabak,
Cawnacome,	Quadaquina,
Obbatinnua,	Huttmoiden,
Nattawahunt,	Apannow,
Caunbatant,	

Young (p. 232) identifies the signers as follows: "Cawnacome was the sachem of Manomet, or Sandwich, Cauhbatant of Mattapoyst or Swanzey, and Chikkatabak, of Neponset. Quadaquina was the brother of Massasoit, and Appann was probably Aspinet, the sachem of Nauset. Obbatinua is supposed to be the same as Obbatinewat, the sachem of Shawmut, or Boston."

16. In the original the word is *Fle,* probably an error in composition for *Ile* or *isle.*

17. Capawak or Nope, Martha's Vineyard.

18. In his *Good News from New England* published in 1624, Winslow corrects this assertion stating, "Whereas myself, and others, in former letters, (which came to the press against my will and knowledge,) wrote that the people about us are a people without any religion, or knowledge of any God, therein I erred, though we could then gather no better; for as they conceive of many divine powers, so of one, whom they call Kiehtan, to be the principal and maker of all the rest, and to be made by none."

19. Winslow brought the first cattle, one bull and three heifers, to Plymouth in 1624.

20. Until recent years lobsters have always been abundant in the area around Plymouth.

21. It should be remembered that the winter of 1620-1621 was relatively mild.

22. An obvious misprint. Young (p. 253) thinks that this should read "other shellfish"; while one writer thinks it might be a misprint for *cockles* and another thinks that the word *clams* should be there.

23. Salad herbs.

24. In the *Relation* the types of grapes are mentioned in detail.

25. Raspberries.

26. Also noted in the *Relation.*

27. In the original the word is *with,* an obvious misprint.

MOURT'S
RELATION:
A JOURNAL
OF THE
PILGRIMS
OF
PLYMOUTH

A LETTER SENT
FROM NEW ENG-
LAND TO A
FRIEND IN
THESE PARTS,
SETTING FORTH A
BRIEF AND TRUE
DECLARATION OF
THE WORTH OF
THAT PLANTA-
TION; AS ALSO
CERTAIN USEFUL
DIRECTIONS FOR
SUCH AS INTEND
A VOYAGE INTO
THOSE PARTS

rivers uninhabited;[28] and withal, to consider those parts of the world wherein you live to be given greatly burdened with abundance of people. These things I thought good to let you understand, being the truth of things as near as I could experimentally take knowledge of, and that you might on our behalf give God thanks, who hath dealt so favorable with us.

Our supply of men from you came the 9th of November, 1621, putting in at Cape Cod, some eight or ten leagues from us.[29] The Indians that dwell thereabouts were they who were owners of the corn which we found in caves, for which we have given them full content,[30] and are in great league with them. They sent us word there was a ship[31] near unto them, but thought it to be a Frenchman; and indeed for ourselves we expected not a friend so soon. But when we perceived that she made for our bay, the governor commanded a great piece to be shot off, to call home such as were abroad at work. Whereupon every man, yea boy, that could handle a gun, were ready, with full resolution that, if she were an enemy, we would stand in our just defense, not fearing them. But God provided better for us than we supposed. These came all in health, not any being sick by the way, otherwise than by seasickness, and so continue at this time, by the blessing of God.[32] The goodwife Ford was delivered of a son the first night she landed,[33] and both of them are very well.

When it pleaseth God we are settled and fitted for the fishing business and other trading, I doubt not but by the blessing of God the gain will give content to all. In the mean time, that we have gotten we have sent by this ship;[34] and though it be not much, yet it will witness for us that we have not been idle, considering the smallness of our number all this summer.[35] We hope the merchants will accept of it, and be encouraged to furnish us with things needful for further employment, which will also encourage us to put forth ourselves to the uttermost.

Now because I expect your coming unto us,[36] with other of our friends, whose company we much desire, I thought good to advertise you of a few things needful.

28. Winslow had noticed the desolation along the banks of the Taunton River in his account of the visit to the *Packanokik*.

29. Young writes (p. 234), "The *Fortune*, a small vessel of 55 tons, brought over Robert Cushman and 35 persons, a part of whom no doubt were the 20 that were put back in the *Speedwell*."

30. The story is told by Bradford in the original *Relation* and by Winslow in his account of the visit to the Nausets.

31. The *Fortune.*

32. The *Fortune* brought thirty-five settlers and Robert Cushman, who returned with her and undoubtedly carried the manuscript of the *Relation* and Winslow's accounts and letter. The persons added were John Adams, William Bassett, William Beale, Edward Bompasse (Bumpers), Jonathan Brewster, son of Elder William Brewster, Clement Briggs, John Cannon, William Conner, Robert Cushman and his son, Thomas, Stephen Dean, Philip de la Noye (Delant), Thomas Havell and his son, Widow Foord (Ford) and three children, William, John, and Martha, Robert Hicks, William Hilton, Bennet Morgan, Thomas Morton, Austin Nicholas, William Palmer and his son, William, William Pitt, Thomas Prence, who later served as governor of the colony, Moses Symonson (Simmons) and probably his wife, Hugh Staire, James Stewart, William Tench, John Winslow, brother of Edward Winslow, and William Wright.

33. The Widow Ford, whose husband died shortly before she left England, had three children with her. There is some conjecture that she married Peter Browne, who came on the *Mayflower*, and that she died or returned to England before 1627.

34. The Pilgrims sent back goods on the *Fortune* to help pay the debt. Robert Cushman was entrusted with the delivery. The ship was captured by a French privateer and the goods were confiscated. Cushman was taken to France as a prisoner and later released.

35. There were only nineteen men in the colony in the summer of 1621.

36. George Morton, to whom this letter is addressed, came to Plymouth on the *Anne* in the spring of 1623.

Be careful to have a very good bread-room to put your biscuits in. Let your cask for beer and water be iron-bound, for the first tier, if not more. Let not your meat be dry-salted; none can better do it than the sailors. Let your meal be so hard trod in your bask that you shall need an adz or hatchet to work it out with. Trust not too much on us for corn at this time, for by reason of this last company that came, depending wholly upon us, we shall have little enough till harvest. Be careful to come by some of your meal to spend by the way; it will much refresh you. Build your cabins as open as you can, and bring good store of clothes and bedding with you. Bring every man a musket or fowling-piece. Let your piece be long in the barrel, and fear not the weight of it, for most of our shooting is from stands. Bring juice of lemons, and take it fasting; it is of good use. For hot water, aniseed water is the best, but use it sparingly. If you bring any thing for comfort in the country, butter or sallet oil, or both, is very good. Our Indian corn, even the coarsest, maketh as pleasant meat as rice; therefore spare that, unless to spend by the way. Bring paper and linseed oil for your windows,[37] with cotton yarn for your lamps. Let your shot be most for big fowls, and bring store of powder and shot. I forbear further to write for the present, hoping to see you by the next return. So I take my leave, commending you to the Lord for a safe conduct unto us, resting in him,

Your loving friend,

E. W.[38]

Plymouth, in New England, this 11th of December, 1621.[39]

MOURT'S RELATION: A JOURNAL OF THE PILGRIMS OF PLYMOUTH

A LETTER SENT FROM NEW ENG-LAND TO A FRIEND IN THESE PARTS, SETTING FORTH A BRIEF AND TRUE DECLARATION OF THE WORTH OF THAT PLANTA-TION; AS ALSO CERTAIN USEFUL DIRECTIONS FOR SUCH AS INTEND A VOYAGE INTO THOSE PARTS

---

37. Young remarks (p. 237), " 'Oiled paper to keep out the snowstorms of a New England winter.' This seems to give us some idea of the exposures and hardships of the first colonists." Dexter (p. 142) refers to the "daubing" between the planks of the houses and asserts that these "give one an idea of the rudeness of the houses of the plantation at this time."

38. Edward Winslow.

39. Tuesday, December 11/21, 1621, exactly one year from the day on which the shallop landed on the shore of Plymouth.

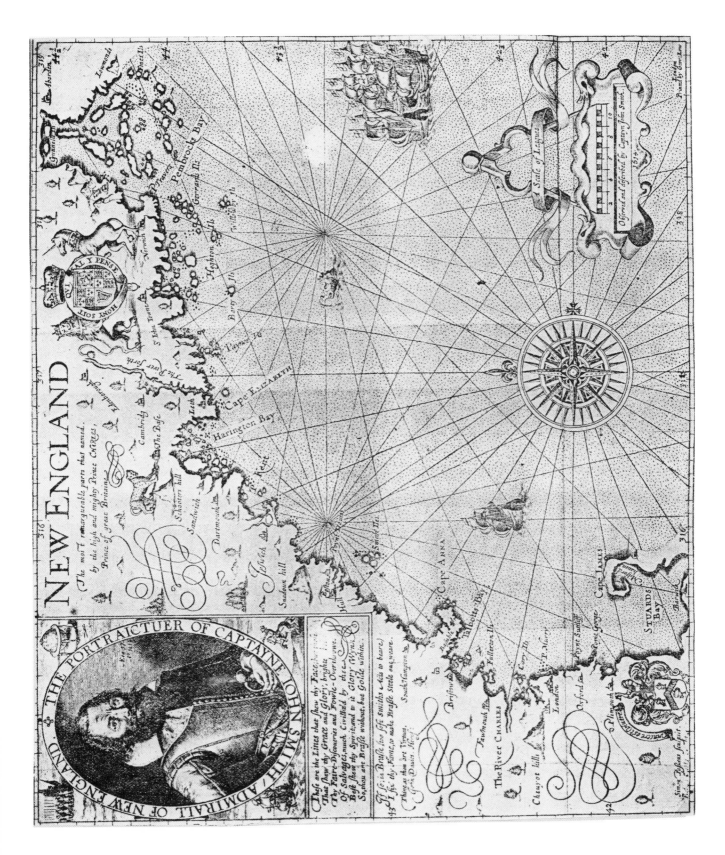

Captain John Smith's Map of New England

Reasons and Considerations Touching the Lawfulness of Removing Out of England Into the Parts of America

FORASMUCH as many exceptions are daily made against the going into and inhabiting of foreign desert places, to the hindrances of plantations abroad, and the increase of distractions at home; it is not amiss that some which have been ear-witnesses of the exceptions made, and are either agents or abettors of such removals and plantations, do seek to give content to the world, in all things that possibly they can.

And although the most of the opposites are such as either dream of raising their fortunes here to that then which there is nothing more unlike, or such as affecting their homeborn country so vehemently, as that they had rather with all their friends, beg, yea, starve in it, than undergo a little difficulty in seeking abroad; yet are there some who, out of doubt in tenderness of conscience, and fear to offend God by running before they are called, are straitened and do straiten others from going to foreign plantations.

For whose cause especially I have been drawn, out of my good affection to them, to publish some reasons that might give them content and satisfaction, and also stay and stop the wilful and witty caviller; and herein I trust I shall not be blamed of any godly wise, though through my slender judgement I should miss the mark, and not strike the nail on the head, considering it is the first attempt that hath been made (that I know of) to defend those enterprises. Reason would, therefore, that if any man of deeper reach and better judgement see further or otherwise, that he rather instruct me than deride me.

And being studious for brevity, we must first consider, that whereas God of old did call and summon our fathers by predictions, dreams, visions, and certain illuminations, to go from their countries, places and habitations, to reside and dwell here and there, and to wander up and down from city to city, and land to land, according to his will and pleasure; now there is no such calling to be expected for any matter whatsoever, neither must any so much as imagine that there will now be any such thing. God did once so train up his people, but now he doth not, but speaks in another manner, and so we must apply ourselves to God's present dealing, and not to

CAUTIONS.
GEN. XII. I.
& 2. &
XXXV. I.
PSALM
CV. I3.
HEB. I. I, 2.

77

JOSH.
V. 12.

his wonted dealing; and as the miracle of giving manna ceased, when the fruits of the land became plenty, so God having such a plentiful storehouse of directions in his holyword, there must not now any extraordinary revelations be expected. But now the ordinary examples and precepts of the Scriptures, reasonably and rightly understood and applied, must be the voice and the word, that must call us, press us, and direct us in every action.

GEN.
XVII. 8.

Neither is there any land or possession now, like unto the possession which the Jews had in Canaan, being legally holy and appropriated unto a holy people, the seed of Abraham, in which they dwelt securely, and had their days prolonged, it being by an immediate voice said, that he (the Lord) gave it them as a land of rest after their weary travels, and a type of eternal rest in heaven. But now there is no land of that sanctimony, no land so appropriated, none typical; much less any that can be said to be given of God to any nation, as was Canaan, which they and their seed must dwell in, till God sendeth upon them sword or captivity. But now we are all, in

2 COR. V.
1, 2, 3.

all places, strangers and pilgrims, travellers and sojourners, most properly, having no dwelling but in this earthen tabernacle; our dwelling is but a wandering, and our abiding but as a fleeting, and in a word our home is nowhere but in the heavens,[1] in that house not made with his hands, whose maker and builder is God, and to which all ascend that love the coming of our Lord Jesus.

Though then there may be reasons to persuade a man to live in this or that land, yet there cannot be the same reasons which the Jews had; but now, as natural, civil and religious hands tie man, so they must be bound, and as good reasons for things terrene and heavenly appear, so they must be led.

OBJECT.

And so here falleth in our question, how a man that is here born and bred, and hath lived some years, may remove himself into another country.

ANS. 1.

I answer, a man must not respect only to live, and do good to himself, but he should see where he can live to do most good to others; for, as one saith, "He whose

WHAT
PERSONS
MAY
HENCE
QUARTER.

living is but for himself, it is time he were head." Some men there are who of necessity must here live, as being tied to duties either to church, commonwealth, household, kindred, &c.; but others, and that many, who do no good in none of those, nor can do none, as being not able, or not in favor, or as wanting opportunity, and live as outcasts—nobodies, eyesores, eating but for themselves, teaching but themselves, and doing good to none, either in soul or body, and so pass over days, years and months, yea, so live and so die. Now such should lift up their eyes and see

WHY THEY
SHOULD
REMOVE.

whether there be not some other place and country to which they may go to do good, and have use towards others of that knowledge, wisdom, humanity, reason, strength, skill, faculty, &c. which God hath given them for the service of others and his own glory.

LUKE
XIX. 20.

But not to pass the bounds of modesty so far as to name any, though I confess I know many, who sit here still with their talent in a napkin, having notable endowments both of body and mind, and might do great good if they were in some places, which here do none, nor can do none, and yet through fleshly fear, niceness, straitness of heart, &c. sit still and look on, and will not hazard a drachim of health, nor a day of pleasure, nor an hour of rest to further the knowledge and salvation of

REAS. 1.

the sons of Adam in that new world, where a drop of the knowledge of Christ is most

---

1. In the margin note the author's observes, "So were the Jews, but yet their temporal blessing and inheritances were more large than ours."

precious, which is here not set by. Now what shall we say to such a profession of Christ, to which is joined no more denial of a man's self?

But some will say, What right have I to go live in the heathens' country?

OBJECT.
ANS.

Letting pass the ancient discoveries, contracts and agreements which our Englishmen have long since made in those parts, together with the acknowledgment of the histories and chronicles of other nations, who profess the land of America from the Cape de Florida unto the Bay of Canada (which is south and north three hundred leagues and upwards, and east and west further than yet hath been discovered) is proper to the king of England, yet letting that pass, lest I be thought to meddle further than it concerns me, or further than I have discerning, I will mention such things as are within my reach, knowledge, sight and practice, since I have travailed in these affairs.

And first, seeing we daily pray for the conversion of the heathens, we must consider whether there be not some ordinary means and course for us to take to convert them, or whether prayer for them be only referred to God's extraordinary work from heaven. Now it seemeth unto me that we ought also to endeavour and use the means to convert them; and the means cannot be used unless we go to them, or they come to us. To us they cannot come, our land is full; to them we may go, their land is empty.

REAS. 2.

That then is sufficient reason to prove our going thither to live, lawful. Their land is spacious and void, and there are few, and do but run over the grass, as do also the foxes and wild beasts. They are not industrious, neither have art, science, skill or faculty to use either the land or the commodities of it; but all spoils, rots, and is marred for want for manuring, gathering, ordering, &c. As the ancient patriarchs, therefore, removed from straiter places into more roomy, where the land lay idle and waste, and none used it, though there dwelt inhabitants by them, as Gen. xiii. 6, 11, 12, and xxxiv. 21, and xii. 20, so is it lawful now to take a land which none useth, and make use of it.

REAS. 3.

And as it is a common land, or unused and undressed country, so we have it by common consent, composition and agreement;[2] which agreement is double. First, the imperial governor, Massasoit, whose circuits, in likelihood, are larger than England and Scotland, hath acknowledged the King's Majesty of England to be his master and commander, and that once in my hearing, yea, and in writing, under his hand, to Captain Standish, both he and many other kings which are under him, as Oamet, Nauset, Cummaquid, Narrowhiggonset, Namaschet, &c., with divers others that dwell about the bays of Patuxet and Massachuset.[3] Neither had this been accomplished by threats and blows, or shaking of sword and sound of trumpet; for as our faculty that way is small, and our strength less, so our warring with them is after another manner, namely, by friendly usage, love, peace, honest and just carriages, good counsel, &c., that so we and they may not only live in peace in that land, and they yield subjection to an earthly prince, but that as voluntaries they may be persuaded at length to embrace the Prince of Peace, Christ Jesus, and rest in peace with him forever.

REAS. 4.

PSAL. CX. 3, & XlVIII. 3.

Secondly, this composition is also more particular and applicatory, as touching ourselves there inhabiting. The emperor, by joint consent, hath promised and ap-

---

2. The writer adds, "This is to be considered as respecting New England, and the territories about its plantation."

3. See the preceding journal and accounts.

MOURT'S
RELATION:
A JOURNAL
OF THE
PILGRIMS OF
PLYMOUTH

REASONS AND
CONSIDERATIONS
TOUCHING THE
LAWFULNESS OF
REMOVING OUT
OF ENGLAND
INTO THE PARTS
OF AMERICA

pointed us to live at peace where we will in all his dominions, taking what place we will, and as much land as we will,[4] and bringing as many people as we will; and that for these two causes. First, because we are the servants of James, king of England, whose the land (as he confesseth) is. Secondly, because he hath found us just, honest, kind and peaceable, and so loves our company. Yea, and that in these things there is no dissimulation on his part, nor fear of breach (except our security engender in them some unthought of treachery, or our uncivility provoke them to anger) is most plain in other Relations,[5] which show that the things they did were more out of love than out of fear.

It being the, first, a vast and empty chaos; secondly, acknowledged the right of our sovereign king; thirdly, by a peaceable composition in part possessed of divers of his loving subjects, I see not who can doubt or call in question the lawfulness of inhabiting or dwelling there; but that it may be as lawful for such as are not tied upon some special occasion here, to live there as well as here. Yea, and as the enterprise is weighty and difficult, so the honor is more worthy, to plant a rude wilderness, to enlarge the honor and fame of our dread sovereign, but chiefly to display the efficacy and power of the Gospel, both in zealous preaching, professing, and wise walking under it, before the faces of these poor blind infidels.

As for such as object the tediousness of the voyage thither, the danger of pirates' robbery, of the savages' treachery, &c., these are but lions in the way; and it were well for such men if they were in heaven. For who can show them a place in this world where iniquity shall not compass them at the heels, and where they shall have a day without grief, or a lease of life for a moment? And who can tell but God, what dangers may lie at our doors, even in our native country, or what plots may be abroad, or when God will cause our sun to go down at noon-day, and, in the midst of our peace and security, lay upon us some lasting scourge for our so long neglect and contempt of his most glorious Gospel?

But we have here great peace, plenty of the Gospel, and many sweet delights and variety of comforts.

True, indeed; and far be it from us to deny and diminish the least of these mercies. But have we rendered unto God thankful obedience for this long peace, whilst other peoples have been at wars? Have we not rather murmured, repined, and fallen at jars amongst ourselves, whilst our peace hath lasted with foreign power? Was there ever more suits in law, more envy, contempt and reproach than nowadays? Abraham and Lot departed asunder when there fell a breach betwixt them, which was occasioned by the straitness of the land; and surely I am persuaded, that howsoever the frailties of men are principal in all contentions, yet the straitness of the place is such, as each man is fain to pluck his means, as it were, out of his neighbour's throat, there is such pressing and oppressing in town and country, about farms,

PROV.
XXII. 13.
PSAL.
XIXI. 5.
MATT. VI.
6:34.
AMOS
VII. 9.

OBJECT.
ANS.
2 CHRO.
XX II.

GEN. XIII,
9, 10.

---

4. Young notes, "In the 'Warrantable Grounds and Proceedings of the First Associates of New Plymouth, in their laying the first foundation of this Government, in their making of laws, and disposing of the lands within the same,' prefixed to the Code of Laws, printed in 1685, it is stated that 'by the favor of the Almighty they began the colony in New England (there being then no other within its said continent) at a place called by the natives Apaum, alias Patuxet, but by the English New Plymouth. All which lands being void of inhabitants, we, the said John Carver, William Bradford, Edward Winslow, William Brewster, Isaac Allerton, and the rest of our associates entering into a league of peace with Massasoit, since called Woodsmequn, prince or sachem of those parts, he, the said Massasoit, freely gave them all the lands adjacent, to them and their heirs forever." (p. 245)
5. The reference is, of course, to the preceding journal.

trades, traffic, &c.; so as a man can hardly any where set up a trade, but he shall pull down two of his neighbours.

The towns abound with young tradesmen, and the hospitals are full of the ancient; the country is replenished with new farmers, and the almshouses are filled with old laborers. Many there are who get their living with bearing burdens; but more are fain to burden the land with their whole bodies. Multitudes get their means of life by prating, and so do numbers more by begging. Neither come these straits upon men always through temperance, ill husbandry, indiscretion, &c., as some think; but even the most wise, sober, and discreet men go often to the wall, when they have done their best; wherein, as God's providence swayeth all, so it is easy to see that the straitness of the place, having in it so many strait hearts, cannot but produce such effects more and more; so as every indifferent minded man should be ready to say with father Abraham, "Take thou the right hand, and I will take the left": let us not oppress, straiten, and afflict one another; but seeing there is a spacious land, the way to which is through the sea, we will end this difference in a day.

That I speak nothing about the bitter contention that hath been about religion, by writing, disputing, and inveighing earnestly one against another, the heat of which zeal, if it were turned against the rude barbarism of the heathens, it might do more good in a day, than it hath done here in many years. Neither of the little love to the Gospel, and profit which is made by the preachers in most places, which might easily drive the zealous to the heathens; who, no doubt, if they had but a drop of that knowledge which here flieth about the streets, would be filled with exceeding great joy and gladness, as that they would even pluck the kingdom of heaven by violence, and take it, as it were, by force.

The greatest let that is yet behind is the sweet fellowship of friends, and the satiety of bodily delights.

But can there be two nearer friends almost than Abraham and Lot, or than Paul and Barnabas? And yet, upon as little occasions as we have here, they departed asunder, two of them being patriarchs of the church of old, the other the apostles of the church which is new; and their covenants were such as it seemeth might bind as much as any covenant between men at this day; and yet to avoid greater inconveniencies, they departed asunder.

Neither must men take so much thought for the flesh, as not to be pleased except they can pamper their bodies with variety of dainties. Nature is content with little, and health is much endangered by mixtures upon the stomach. The delights of the palate do often inflame the vital parts; as the tongue setteth afire the whole body. Secondly, varieties here are not common to all, but many good men are glad to snap at a crust. The rent-taker lives on sweet morsels, but the rent-payer eats a dry crust often with watery eyes; and it is nothing to say what some one of a hundred hath; which I warrant you is short enough.

And they also which now live so sweetly, hardly will their children attain to that privilege; but some circumventor or other will outstrip them, and make them sit in the dust, to which men are brought in one age, but cannot get out of it again in seven generations.

To conclude, without all partiality, the present consumption which groweth upon us here, whilst the land groaneth under so many close-fisted and unmerciful men, being compared with the easiness, plainness and plentifulness in living in those

REASONS AND CONSIDERATIONS TOUCHING THE LAWFULNESS OF REMOVING OUT OF ENGLAND INTO THE PARTS OF AMERICA

THE LAST LET.

JAMES III. 6.

MOURT'S
RELATION:
A JOURNAL
OF THE
PILGRIMS OF
PLYMOUTH

REASONS AND
CONSIDERATIONS
TOUCHING THE
LAWFULNESS OF
REMOVING OUT
OF ENGLAND
INTO THE PARTS
OF AMERICA

remote places, may quickly persuade any man to a liking of this course, and to practice as removal; which being done by honest, godly and industrious men, they shall there be right heartily welcome; but for other of dissolute and profane life, their rooms are better than companies. For if here, where the Gospel hath been so long and plentifully taught, they are yet frequent in such vices as the heathen would shame to speak of, what will they be when there is less restraint in word and deed? My only suit to all men is, that whether they live there or here, they would learn to use this world as they used it not, keeping faith and a good conscience, both with God and men, that when the day of account shall come, they may come forth as good and fruitful servants, and freely be received, and enter into the joy of their Master.

R. C.[6]

---

6. R. C. is Robert Cushman, a leader in the Leyden Congregation. He was twice sent from Leyden to England to take part in the negotiations preceding the Pilgrim's emigration. He was aboard the *Speedwell* in 1620 but was obliged to turn back. He came over on the *Fortune* in the fall of 1621 with his son Thomas and stayed one month. His son was left in William Bradford's care. He returned on the *Fortune* on December 13/23, 1621, undoubtedly carrying with him this *Relation* and *Journal*. Cushman was detained at Ile-d'Yeu after the capture of the *Fortune* by the French and reached London on February 17/27, 1622.

THE EARLY SETTLERS

Mayflower PASSENGERS
1620

*INDICATES DIED FIRST WINTER

John Alden

Isaac Allerton
    *Mary (Morris) Allerton, *his wife*
    Bartholomew Allerton, *son*
    Remember Allerton, *son*
    Mary Allerton, *daughter*

John Allerton or Alderton

John Billington
    Ellen Billington, *his wife*
    Francis Billington, *son*
    John Billington, *son*

William Bradford
    *Dorothy (May) Bradford, *his wife*

*Richard Britteridge

William Brewster
    Mary Brewster, *his wife*
    Love Brewster, *son*
    Wrestling Brewster, *son*

Peter Browne

*William Button

*Robert Carter

*John Carver
    *Catherine Carver, *his wife*
    *_____, *female maid-servant*

*James Chilton
    *Mrs. _____ Chilton, *his wife*
    Mary Chilton, *daughter*

*Richard Clarke

Francis Cooke
    John Cooke, *son*

Humility Cooper

Edward Dotey

*John Crackston
    John Crackston, *son*

Francis Eaton
    *Sarah Eaton, *his wife*
    Samuel Eaton, *son*

_____ Ellis

*Thomas English

*Moses Fletcher

MOURT'S
RELATION:
A JOURNAL
OF THE
PILGRIMS OF
PLYMOUTH

THE EARLY
SETTLERS

Mayflower
PASSENGERS
1620

Edward Fuller
    Mrs. Ann Fuller, *his wife*
    Samuel Fuller, *son*

Samuel Fuller, *surgeon*

*Richard Gardiner

*John Goodman

*William Holbeck

*John Hooke

Stephen Hopkins
    Elizabeth Hopkins, *his wife*
    Giles Hopkins, *son*
    Constance Hopkins, *daughter*
    Damaris Hopkins
    Oceanus Hopkins

John Howland

*John Langemore

William Latham

Edward Leister

*Edmund Margeson

*Christopher Martin
    *Mrs. _____ Martin, *his wife*

Desire Minter

*Ellen More

*Jasper More

Richard More

_____ More

*William Mullins
    *Alice Mullins, *his wife*
    *Joseph Mullins, *son*
    Priscilla Mullins, *daughter*

*Degory Priest

Solomon Prower

*John Rigdale
    *Alice Rigdale, *his wife*

*Thomas Rogers
    Joseph Rogers, *his son*

Henry Samson

George Soule

Miles Standish
    Rose Standish, *his wife*

*Elias Story

*Edward Thompson

*Edward Tilley
    *Anne Tilley, *his wife*

*John Tilley
    *Elizabeth Tilley, *his wife*
    Elizabeth Tilley, *daughter*

*Thomas Tinker
    *Mrs. _____ Tinker, *his wife*
    * _____ Tinker, *son*

William Trevore

*John Turner
    * _____ Turner, *son*
    * _____ Turner, *son*

Richard Warren

*William White
    Susanna Fuller White, *his wife*
    Resolved White, *son*
    Peregrine White, *son, born
        on Mayflower*

*Roger Wilder

*Thomas Williams

Edward Winslow
    Elizabeth Winslow, *his wife*

Gilbert Winslow

Fortune PASSENGERS
NOVEMBER 1621

John Adams

William Bassett
    Mrs. Elizabeth Bassett, *his wife*

William Beale

Edward Bompass (Bumpers, Bumpas)

Jonathan Brewster

Clement Briggs

John Cannon

William Conner

Robert Cushman
    Thomas Cushman, *his son*

Stephen Deane

Phillippe De La Noye

Thomas Flavell
    _____, *his son*

Mrs. Martha Ford
    William Ford, *son*
    Martha Ford, *daughter*
    John Ford, *son*

Robert Hicks

William Hilton

Benedict Morgan

Thomas Morton

Austin Nicholas

William Palmer
    William, *his son*

William Pitt

Thomas Prence

Hugh Stacey

James Steward

Moses Symonson (Simmons)

William Tench

John Winslow

William Wright
    Mrs. Priscilla Wright, *his wife*

SIGNERS OF THE MAYFLOWER COMPACT

(SOURCE—NATHANIEL MORTON, *New Englands Memoriall* [1669])

John Carver

William Bradford

Edward Winslow

William Brewster

Isaac Allerton

Myles Standish

John Alden

Samuel Fuller

Christopher Martin

William Mullins

William White

Richard Warren

John Howland

Stephen Hopkins

Edward Tilley

John Tilley

Francis Cooke

Thomas Rogers

Thomas Tinker

John Rigdale

Edward Fuller

John Turner

Francis Eaton

James Chilton

John Crackston

John Billington

Moses Fletcher

John Goodman

Degory Priest

Thomas Williams

Gilbert Winslow

Edmund Margeson

Peter Browne

Richard Britteridge

George Soule

Richard Clarke

Richard Gardiner

John Allerton

Thomas English

Edward Dotey

Edward Leister

BIBLIOGRAPHICAL NOTE

Although a large number of secondary works have been consulted in the preparation of this edition of *Mourt's Relation*, four books have been used extensively for the documents they provided. They are

Arber, Edward. *The Story of the Pilgrim Fathers, 1606-1623 A.D.;* as told by Themselves, Their Friends, and Their Enemies. Boston: Houghton Mifflin Company, 1897.

Dexter, Henry Martyn, ed. *Mourt's Relation or Journal of the Pilgrims at Plymouth.* Boston: J. K. Wiggin, 1865.

Freeman, Frederick. *The History of Cape Cod, etc.* Boston: Geo. C. Rand and Avery, 1858-1862. 2 vols.

Young, Alexander, ed. *Chronicles of the Pilgrim Fathers of the Colony of Plymouth, from 1602 to 1625.* Boston: C. C. Little and J. Brown, 1841.

A Few Words About
Dr. Jordan D. Fiore

Dr. Jordan D. Fiore's labor of love, this modern edition of *Mourt's Relation,* is an achievement of scholarship which grew out of his dedication to demonstrating the relevance of the Pilgrim experience to Twentieth Century Americans.

Dr. Fiore's talents as a racounteur often spurs students, readers, and listeners to an interest in historical topics. However, it is his impeccable scholarship which challenges them to use history as a tool for understanding themselves, and their place in destiny.

He has given generations of students, in the public schools of Fall River and Swansea, Massachusetts, at the University of Rhode Island, at Boston University, and most of all at Bridgewater State College, a powerful example of excellence in scholarship and teaching. Multiple scholarly and popular publications, and hundreds of lectures, attest to his determination to communicate enthusiasm for the study of history to a broad audience. His topics have ranged from American colonial and revolutionary history, Massachusetts government, American diplomat Francis Baylies, Abraham Lincoln and the Civil War, to Lizzie Borden, the history of Portugal, book collecting, and current affairs.

Dr. Fiore is a native son of Fall River, Massachusetts, where members of his family have been active in civil, musical and church affairs. An honor graduate of Fall River's B.M.C. Durfee High School, he received a Bachelor of Science degree from Bridgewater State College in 1940. After serving in the United States Army in World War II, he went on to earn a Master of Arts degree in English from Boston University Graduate School in 1946 and a Doctor of Philosophy degree in History in 1950. His graduate studies included work done at Brown University and New York University Graduate Schools.

He is a long-time resident of Taunton, Massachusetts, where he has been deeply involved in civic affairs. During eight years as an elected member of the Taunton School Committee, including two years as chairman, he was a staunch advocate of

MOURT'S
RELATION:
A JOURNAL
OF THE
PILGRIMS OF
PLYMOUTH

A FEW
WORDS ABOUT
DR. JORDAN D.
FIORE

academic excellence in public schools. The Taunton Jaycees named him Educator of the Year in 1975, and his *alma mater* bestowed upon him the Nicholas Tillinghast Award for distinguished service to education. He is currently president of Taunton's Old Colony Historical Society.

State and national projects have also called for his services. He has been an active member of the Advisory Committee of the Massachusetts Civil War Centennial Commission and the Massachusetts Bicentennial Commission. From 1970-1976, he served as an advisor to the National Archives Regional Commission.

His wide range of interests is reflected in his memberships, which include the Board of Directors of the Plymouth Rock Foundation, the Pilgrim Society, of which he is a Trustee and former member of the Executive Board, the Civil War Round Table of Boston, The Lincoln Group of Boston, of which he is vice-president, and the Coimbra Club, an organization devoted to the study of Portuguese culture.

The Pilgrim fathers strove to turn a wilderness into a community in which they and their children could live out their destiny and their salvation in dignity, peace and honor. Although they might view some aspects of that community today with surprise or even dismay, they would be proud to find scholars, teachers and citizens of Dr. Fiore's caliber putting their history to work in the last quarter of the Twentieth Century.

JEAN STONEHOUSE
Assistant Professor, History
Bridgewater State College

A Few Words About the Plymouth Rock Foundation

The Plymouth Rock Foundation is an uncompromising advocate of Biblical principles of self and civil government and the Christian world and life view. It is an expositor of the Bible-based principle approach to education in the Christian school and the Christian home and in that effort sponsors seminars for Christian educators and pastors. Also, the Foundation seeks to acquaint today's Americans with the blessings and facts of the nation's Christian heritage, thus to help undo and eradicate the harm that has been done by the uninformed and the revisionists who would discredit or deny the Biblical foundations of the American Republic.

The Plymouth Rock Foundation's publishes several periodicals: the LETTER FROM PLYMOUTH ROCK and the *FAC-Sheet*.

These publications are sent regularly to the thousands of Christian schools, churches and families in the United States and 14 foreign nations that comprise the Foundation's "Pilgrim Family." To date, more than 5 million copies of various *FAC-Sheets* and approximately 1 million copies of *Letters From Plymouth Rock* have been produced and distributed to and through that "Family."

In addition to those periodicals, Plymouth Rock also produces books and audio-visual materials (audio and video tapes, etc.) as part of its work for the reconstruction of America's Biblical foundations.

Plymouth Rock is a non-denominational, non-profit, public foundation (Section 501 [c] 3). It was incorporated in the Commonwealth of Massachusetts in 1970, A.D. Financial support for its ministry comes solely from those who are led by The Lord to share with it some of that which He has entrusted to them. The United States Department of the Treasury has deemed such contributions to be tax deductible, should the donor be so inclined.

For further information concerning the Plymouth Rock Foundation and its programs and publications and other materials, please contact our General Offices in Marlborough, NH, 03455.

JOHN G. TALCOTT, JR.
President

RUS WALTON
Executive Director

INDEX

95

MOURT'S
RELATION:
A JOURNAL
OF THE
PILGRIMS
OF
PLYMOUTH

INDEX

MOURT'S
RELATION:
A JOURNAL
OF THE
PILGRIMS OF
PLYMOUTH

INDEX

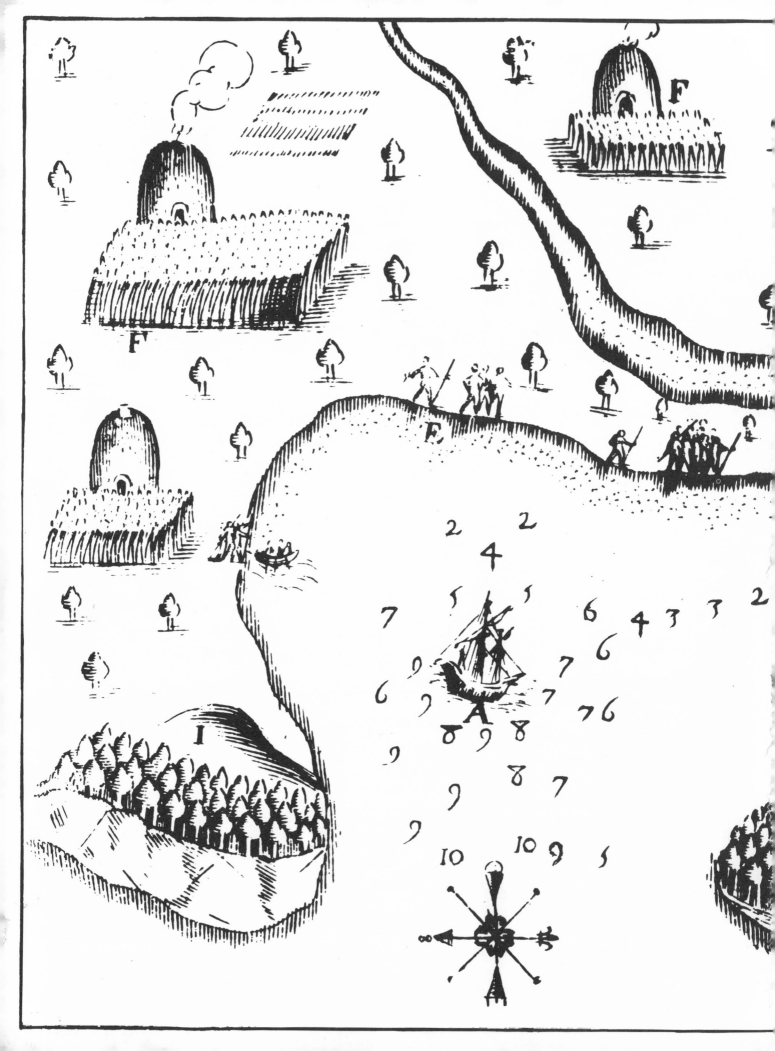